Two Old Ladies
SMILING

A Journey to My Place of Blessing

Michael Cook

WESTBOW
PRESS®
A DIVISION OF THOMAS NELSON
& ZONDERVAN

This book is a work of non-fiction. Unless otherwise noted, the author and the publisher make no explicit guarantees as to the accuracy of the information contained in this book and in some cases, names of people and places have been altered to protect their privacy.

Scripture taken from the King James Version of the Bible.

WestBow Press books may be ordered through booksellers or by contacting:

WestBow Press
A Division of Thomas Nelson & Zondervan
1663 Liberty Drive
Bloomington, IN 47403
www.westbowpress.com
1 (866) 928-1240

Because of the dynamic nature of the Internet, any web addresses or links contained in this book may have changed since publication and may no longer be valid. The views expressed in this work are solely those of the author and do not necessarily reflect the views of the publisher, and the publisher hereby disclaims any responsibility for them.

Any people depicted in stock imagery provided by Thinkstock are models, and such images are being used for illustrative purposes only. Certain stock imagery © Thinkstock.

ISBN: 978-1-5127-9855-5 (sc)
ISBN: 978-1-5127-9854-8 (e)

Library of Congress Control Number: 2017912331

Print information available on the last page.

WestBow Press rev. date: 08/31/2017

Loving His children; building His church

Foreword

As I chatted with my wife Sue regarding the general content and purpose of this book, she asked all of the proper questions. She only recently completed her book *Allow The Children,* which is a history through the year 2015 of the 501(c)3 organization that the Lord has privileged us to found and shepherd for these past fourteen plus years. Allow The Children was founded with the premise that "Our mission is to be used by God as He answers the cries of the lost and helpless children of the world." To that end, Sue and I have come alongside Christ Followers in a number of countries, to help them help their children, and to help them strengthen their churches and fellowships. Sue asked me a question which caused me to struggle a bit. "What is your purpose for writing the book?" I ordinarily like to be able to answer such queries with a short, concise response, that is initiated and crafted from the reasoning and intellectual portions of my brain. However, my first thoughts of crafting this tome were from the *emotional* part of my brain. I desired to honor my parents and acknowledge the role they played in my life. I also wanted to honor God and give Him my praise for all He has enabled me to be a part of over the years. As the various sections of this book have flowed from my brain, however, it seems that I am writing a lot about personal struggles. It is interesting that both the most atheistic of the existentialists and the most God fearing of the theologians would agree that life consists of many struggles. The existentialist ultimately wants to escape this life of struggles, while the theologian champions the overcoming of struggles through the Word of God and the grace and faith given us by the Almighty.

I worked with missionaries for sixteen years as the Missions Committee chairman of my church. I watched from the sidelines as they faced many difficult struggles. One of the most excruciating of these struggles was what to do when an aging parent needed help, yet the missionary felt called by God to be ten thousand miles away sharing the Gospel. There were varying degrees of struggle, arising from the availability or lack of a sibling group who might be active in helping the aging parent. If one had a sister or brother who assumed the role of caregiver/helper, then it was easier to make the decision to go abroad for an extended length of time, then return home to give the caregiving sibling a break. If the missionary was an only child, or his siblings were unable to care for their parents, the decision was a very difficult one. I lived through this later scenario for a few years, and had to make the decision to forgo most of my overseas time, in order to help my aging parents. The pain from these kinds of struggles is very personal, and does not get discussed. Even after one decides to fill the caregiver role, he finds himself with a new set of struggles about how much or how little he needs to be doing. Can the parent live alone? Can the parent still drive? What kind of medical treatment does the parent need? Can the parent still make financial decisions by himself? The list goes on and on. There are not always good solid black and white answers to these questions. I thought it might be helpful to some people going through this to know that thousands of us are struggling with the same issues every day. I suppose that answers Sue's question, and is one of my major purposes in writing this book.

As missionaries, we also have struggles within our ministries. If we believe that there is an adversary who actively opposes the Gospel, then we also must be ready to face obstacles and adversity as we pursue our God given ministry. If we believe that God is doing His work, and we are a servant doing His bidding, then we must be willing to trust Him when things are going well, and when things are falling apart. Our ministry has had its ups and downs over the years. We have faced everything from armed insurrections in our countries to betrayal by people we loved and trusted. We have seen God overcome impossible obstacles, and we have felt the sting of God's chastening when we veered off of His course and onto a path of our own choosing.

One of the advantages of being older is that we have a big picture frame of reference. We have walked through adversity and seen the Lord sustain us. We have stood on the mountain tops and shouted praise to the Lord in times of great spiritual victories. We have knelt and cried out to God in the valley of despair. We have trusted the Lord, and found Him to be true to His word. The corresponding disadvantage of being older is that we have put out of our minds what it was like to be young and wondering what God's will was for our lives. We don't like to recall the false starts and the retracing of steps on our journey toward God's place of blessing for us. The process of learning to depend on God rather than on self can be a painful one. It is a source of shame when we think of the times we grumbled against God's provision rather than giving thanks for His presence.

We all seem to do our wilderness experience like the Israelites in the book of Exodus. Even when we are well on our way to God's place of blessing for our lives, we look back and long for what we thought was good in the life we had before God called us. Like the Israelites, we also get weighed down by our focus on our circumstances, rather than on God. We need that continued exhortation to stop our struggling: "*Be still, and know that I am God. I will be exalted among the heathen, I will be exalted in the earth.*" (Psalm 46:10 KJV) We are not promised a journey without difficulties. We are promised a journey that will bring us into God's place of blessing. Israel went into a geographical location, but their real place of blessing came when they were fully surrendered to God's sovereignty in their lives. Only then did they see great obstacles melt away from their path, and great armies flee from them in terror. As we abide in Christ, our place of blessing, we become acutely aware of just how powerful God is, and how powerless we are without Him.

I hope that this book is an encouragement to those coming behind me, who have stepped out to serve the Lord. I am, in a sense, writing memoir, but I don't intend it to be about me. After all, who is Mike Cook? I am nothing more than a man who has tasted and seen that the Lord is good. In writing this book, my purpose is to record the work of the Almighty in the life of one of His most reluctant servants. I have seen the needy helped in over a dozen countries. I have rejoiced over hundreds of villages being reached with the Gospel for the very first time. I have seen churches spring up in these villages, in a manner that only could be credited to the Hand of Providence. I have broken bread with Christ Followers in humble city flats and in run-down huts in remote villages. I have had brothers and sisters in Christ from four continents on their knees in prayer for me when I was experiencing health issues. I have watched little children grow up in our sponsorship program, and become solid members of their communities and churches. I have been privileged to teach hundreds of pastors, who literally took what I taught back to their villages and used it in discipling their church members. I have fellowshipped with men who had been imprisoned, beaten, and threatened with death for their faith. I have experienced unbelievable blessing in this life. *None of this* is attributable to me or my wisdom and strength. I merely showed up at God's appointed times. He chose me generations before I was born. I often like to joke that I was chosen to show just how great God is. If He can use someone like me, He can use anybody to do His bidding. Indeed, as I write, I am relating things from my perspective, and I will most certainly fail to exalt the name of the Lord as much as it should be exalted. I will, however, try to share on all levels. I tend to err on the side of the rational, but I am writing that which is emotional to me. Our lives consist of both intellectual and emotional components, and we dare not deny either.

One final purpose I have for writing this book is that all of us who share in the experience of the book can look at what God has uniquely prepared and positioned us to do. Our family, our environment, our struggles in life, and our time in God's word and prayer, have all played a role in making us who we are. We need to see the Hand of God in our lives each day. In revealing so much of my life and my struggles, I hope to encourage those coming behind me to be faithful to this God who has done so much for me. I believe with all of my heart that the Lord has a purpose for each of His people, and that He is working all things together for the good of that purpose in the life of that person. My journey is simply that: *my journey*. God's purposes for me were not meant to be imposed upon anyone else. As I track various events on my timeline, the purposeful hand of the Almighty is evident. God brought the right people at the right time to encourage me or to challenge me, whichever was needed. I pray that readers of this book will grow to appreciate the purposes of God in their lives, and rejoice in knowing that one far greater than we is guiding our journey.

The Converging Paths

January 2, 1996 was to be the beginning of a journey. In my mind, it was the reality of my first journey to Asia. I had no way of knowing that God was also starting me on a new leg of my life's journey, which would come to define who I am, and what God's purposes are for my life. I arose before four o'clock that morning, had a quiet time, showered, and was rechecking everything in my mind, to be certain I had all that I needed to survive three weeks in Asia.

Sue and I were to be picked up and driven to the Roanoke airport by a man from our church. From there we would go to Detroit, then to Tokyo, and finally to Bangkok, Thailand, which would be our base of operations for ministry in Viet Nam, Nepal, and the Laos/Thailand border area. Sue and I would separate in Bangkok. She would spend three weeks with a team doing medical clinics in small villages at the Laos/Thailand border. I would be part of a team connecting with the underground church in Viet Nam, and with any Christians we could find in the Hindu Kingdom of Nepal. I would join Sue during my third week in Asia, to teach, encourage, and be a helper to the medical teams.

Having served as the mission committee chairman at my church for several years, I had visited some mission fields as a part of knowing and better understanding our missionaries. This trip would expose me to frontier missions. I would visit people who were totally unreached by the gospel. I would visit others who were enduring persecution, even to the threat of death, because of their faith in Christ. My sense was that the understanding I would bring back to our church from these places was a vital part of what God wanted us to be doing. Ever the administrator, I planned on viewing the trip largely as an observer, rather than as a "hands-on" participant.

The phone rang as we waited for our ride. I expected it to be the driver saying he was running a little late. Instead, it was my dad. He told me that my grandfather had passed away during the night. Since my grandfather was in a long-term care facility, following a massive stroke, his passing was not a surprise. I was left with a difficult decision, however. Should I go on to the airport, or should I stay to be with my mother and grandmother for the funeral? I called them both. They were unhesitating in their reply-they wanted me to go. At the time, I really had not considered how much they wanted to see me involved in mission work. I had no intention of changing direction in life. After all, I was very active at my church; helping many missionaries to do their jobs better. Now, looking back, I understand that they saw what God was doing in my life, and were very pleased with it. Both my mother and grandmother (Nanny) had invested many hours telling me Bible stories, reading scripture to me, helping me to memorize verses for Sunday school, and praying with me. I was well aware of how they both reached out to missionaries who were home on furlough. We housed and fed many a traveling missionary speaker when I was growing up, but it never occurred to me what a special opportunity that was for me. With the blessing and encouragement of both of these dear ladies, I set out for Asia.

My eighty-four-year-old grandmother was now a widow for the second time in her life, and my sixty-six-year-old mother was left fatherless for the second time in her life. How the memories of sixty years earlier must have come racing back into their minds that morning. All of my family tree has its roots in Madison County, North Carolina. This area was the poorest county in the state for many years. It was a destitute mountain region in the heart of Appalachia. My mother was born at home right at the beginning of the Great Depression, to a share cropper and his young wife. Weighing in at just over two pounds, there was practically no chance that she would survive without medical care, a neonatal unit or even a warming light.

My grandmother had been a young teenager when she entered an arranged marriage with a man nearly twice her age. She had cared for younger siblings in her large family at home, but had experienced nothing that could prepare her for what she was now facing. An added hindrance to all of this was the demanding, drunken, mountain man husband who was often abusive to this young wife and mother. He had already raised three children with his first wife who had passed away. Even though Nanny was giving herself to helping their daughter survive, he followed his own agenda, and didn't seem to care what his wife wanted to do. My grandmother loved her little girl more than she loved her own life. She very resourcefully kept that tiny baby warm and secure. She kept the baby inside of her shirt next to her skin, to keep the baby at just the right temperature. Because the baby lacked the strength to suck, Nanny dripped milk drop by drop into the baby's mouth. Beyond all expectations, the little baby girl survived. As I think about this story, it becomes very clear to me that the hand of God was at work in my life, years before I ever existed. Obviously, if my mother had not been spared by the Almighty, I would not exist!

My mother grew from a baby into a little girl. Having been so greatly under-sized at birth, she had a lot of catching up to do. Her father continued his drunken ways. Many times my grandmother would step between this raging man and her little girl. My grandmother has always been a woman of prayer and great faith, and she cried out daily to the Lord, begging Him to take her and her daughter out of their terrible situation.

Just after my mother turned seven years old, God answered Nanny's prayer. One evening, in a drunken rage, her husband left the house with his shotgun. His intent was to settle a feud with another man in the style that was common among mountain men in Madison County. Though it had earned the nickname "Bloody Madison" during the Civil War, the county regularly reinforced that image with each passing year. The other man, who set out that night, lay in wait by the path around the mountain. With powerful blasts from his own shotgun, he answered the prayers of my grandmother. She and my mother were now free from the husband and father under whom they had suffered.

The testing of their faith was not over for my mother and grandmother.

It was just ramping up to the next level. As the family of a share cropper, they lived in the house allotted to the man who would work the fields and generate an income for the land owner. With planting season just around the corner, it was imperative that the land owner act quickly to replace the tenant who had been killed. This meant that my mother and grandmother were not only without a bread winner, they were homeless as well. They had very few possessions. The most prominent thing my grandmother inherited was the shotgun that her husband had been carrying the night that he was killed. It had marks on the wooden stock where some of the buck shot had hit it. Our family still owns that antique shotgun. When I see it, I am reminded of where my roots are, and what terrible struggles my mother and grandmother experienced. I grew up hearing the expression, "It is always the darkest before the dawn." Intellectually, I understood it, but Mom and Nanny understood it by experience.

Alone, homeless, and destitute, they had few options. My grandmother took a job as a housekeeper for a local mercantile owner and his wife. She was up well before daylight and the last in bed at night, doing all of the household chores, gardening and caregiving for the children of her employers. She, in turn, received room and board for herself and her daughter. My grandmother's faith was not moved, and she began to pray daily, thanking God for His provision, and asking Him for things for her little girl. Most of my mother's early dresses were made from emptied feed sacks. My grandmother deftly crafted these sacks into proper covering for her child. She also collected every piece of scrap cloth she could lay hold of, and turned them into beautiful quilts for warmth. Essentials like shoes and coats were also cobbled together any way they could. Toys were not affordable. Books were unavailable, except for a Bible and a few cookbooks in the house. These became my mother's friends, and she developed as a phenomenal cook, an excellent reader, and a godly woman-no doubt from her early focus and interest in the available books.

The adversity shared by my mother and grandmother during these difficult years had a profound effect on their lives, especially on their relationship with each other. There was no way any two human beings could have been closer than these two were. I have always thought of them as a matching set. They had the ability to know and understand each other's feelings without saying a word. Whenever one would enter the room where the other was, both their faces would light up in a loving smile. Their relationship was formed and strengthened in the fires of adversity, and it was a very important part of who they were and what they wanted in life. Neither of them had a desire for great wealth. The fact that they had each other was enough. I was well up in years before I grasped this fully. God created these two knowing the role they would play in my life, and in the lives of so many others they would bless during their life time. I was raised under the loving care of both of these great ladies, and can only thank God for their influence on my life.

As I traveled for my first Asian experience, I had no idea how much my life was going to change. We reached Bangkok, Thailand late at night, and checked into a guest house near midnight. At 7:00 a.m., I was standing at the airport preparing to board a flight for Ho Chi Minh City, Viet Nam. At the time, Viet Nam was still a tightly controlled, Communist nation and part of the infamous "Bamboo Curtain" which shut the world out and the citizens in.

The mission of the team with which I was traveling had several aspects. A big part of it was to meet underground church leaders, encourage them, and see how we might help them with their ministry. Another part of our mission was to take Bibles and training materials to them. This meant carrying these materials through the border crossing, risking detection and whatever penalty might befall. To say that I was anxious about this does not capture the fullness of my emotion. Faith shines its brightest when it goes through the fires of testing, and my faith was being tested. As we awaited our boarding, an airline worker came to us and quite unexpectedly, upgraded our whole team to first class. This has only happened to me one other time in over twenty years of international flying. On our two hour flight, first class wasn't that great, but it was a gift from God that reversed a lot of anxiety for the team. It helped as we listened to the instructions of our team leader about going through immigration and customs at Ho Chi Minh City. We would not go in as a group, but would spread out and all go through different lines. If one member of the team was detained, all of the others would continue through without him. This was anxiety producing while we sat in the Bangkok Airport, but it was downright terrifying when we deplaned in Ho Chi Minh City. I had two shoulder bags. One contained my personal effects and the other had training materials for the underground church. As I moved forward in my line, my fear meter was off the charts. Yes, I know, "Be strong and of good courage, neither be afraid…" I was afraid! I reached the front of the line and handed my passport to the glaring policeman at the desk. She took what seemed like an eternity to look through various records and compare them to my documents. Several times she looked directly at me and seemed to be very angry. I was pretty certain that she was going to pull me out of line and I would be in jail very soon. At long last she made eye contact with me, and gruffly inquired, "Where will you be staying while you are in Viet Nam?" This should have been an easy question, but only one member of the team knew this, for security reasons. We were meeting underground church leaders there, and could not have it staked out by the police who were trying to stamp out Christianity in the regime. I answered the question weakly, "In a hotel." It was a good true answer, but did not meet the prescribed guidelines she required. She looked back through papers, shuffled things around, and wrote down something on the application for a visa I had given her. She then sternly looked me in the eye again and said one word in a commanding voice: "Hilton!" With that she handed me my passport and visa, and motioned me on through. "Thank you ma'am," was my vocalization, but my heart was crying out, "Thank you Lord!"

Our team consisted of five men and one woman who was the wife of one of the men. The team leader was a full- time missionary, but the rest of us were all traveling to get a better understanding of what ministry looked like in countries that were considered "closed to the gospel." As a side note, every one of us would go on to serve in missions in an Asian country. This trip was a turning point in the lives of five Americans who had met a Divine appointment in Asia.

The very first cultural lesson we learned was what the Vietnamese thought of Americans. We checked in at our hotel and went across the street to a restaurant for dinner. Kathy, our female team mate, passed on dinner to turn in early because of jet lag. At the restaurant, the proprietor quickly ushered us into a large back room that had seating for over a dozen people around a table. None of us spoke Vietnamese, and the people at the restaurant spoke very broken English. After struggling through giving our orders, we were settling in to wait on the food, when the proprietor came back and told us that the women would be here shortly. Long story short, he was making arrangements for call girls, because that was what he thought American men traveling in Viet Nam would want. We quickly canceled that order. I also learned an important lesson that evening about my system and travel. When I travel far enough to have jet lag, I cannot stay awake past six in the evening. I literally fell asleep in the middle of the meal.

As morning broke, we had all been awake for some time. Not only will jet lag put the traveler to sleep early in the evening, it will make him wide awake very early in the morning. I was awake and reading my Bible by 2:30 a.m. This did not disturb my roommate, Gary, who was wide awake as well. At daylight, we went down and bought coffee and freshly baked French bread from the street vendors. Morning meals in Viet Nam would be my favorite over the many years that I would travel there. Lunches and dinners would prove a bit more adventurous.

We met up with our translator and the lead pastor of a Vietnamese church group. These two remarkable servants of God would be our guides, and for me, cultural mentors. We had a van with its driver meet us in front of the hotel. We loaded six Americans, our translator, the pastor and the driver into a small Asian van. None of the Americans was especially small, and two of our men were quite tall. It seemed a bit of a squeeze, but we had everyone in and settled, or so we thought. We set our course for the hill country to visit several pastors who had undergone great persecution for their faith. We stopped several times along the road, and picked up other pastors who wanted to travel with us. Before our jaunt was over, we had fourteen people in what Americans would call a six passenger van. I learned that day that in Asia, there is always room for another passenger. (I have since been in such a van with sixteen passengers inside and two on the roof.)

We spent much of the day hearing the testimonies of several pastors. These men had served a combined total of over eighty years in prison for preaching the Word of God. They had their houses and land confiscated, and they were left weak and destitute. Despite this, their joy level was much greater than mine. They did not complain about their suffering and were prepared to face more. As we headed back, the lead pastor had the driver stop by a small house. The resident of this house was the widow of a pastor who had died in prison. As the pastor and the lady conversed in Vietnamese, I felt a strong prompting in my heart to give the lady the money in my front pocket. This was sixty dollars which I had separated out for easy access in case I wanted to buy something. I had other cash with me, but this strong prompting was to put my hand in this pocket, take out the bills and give them to the lady. I did this by first giving it to the pastor as an intermediary and translator. The lady got tears in her eyes and said something to the pastor. He translated for me. "This lady ran out of food and money several days ago. She has been crying out to God to send help to her, and God sent you!" I still get chills thinking about this today. God had put me on a plane and had flown me twelve thousand miles around the globe, had put money in my pocket, and had prompted me to give it to this lady, who had been on her knees asking for it. I always believed in my intellect that God could do something this amazing. I also knew from Scripture that God often answered one person's prayer by sending another person to minister. Finding myself right in the midst of it happening, however, opened my faith to a whole new perspective. One of the biggest steps in trusting God is believing not only that He *can* do something, but that *He will do it*. I had not done anything great. This small ministry did not require any special skills. I was a business man, and the money was not a big sacrifice for me. There were hundreds of thousands of godly men more worthy than I to be given the privilege of serving in this capacity, yet there I was, experiencing God in a very special way. I would remember this experience seven years later when it would be repeated in Nepal, at the next big turning point of my life.

We visited more pastors the next day. We stopped at what used to be called a filling station in the United States when I was growing up.

A couple of gas pumps and lots of tools for fixing flat tires or repairing other maladies of cars were basically all that was there. The owners of this place were Christians and were delighted to have the visiting Americans. They hustled around and came up with some large bottles of Pepsi. I had been very uneasy about various things we were eating and drinking on this trip. As someone who was in the restaurant industry, I had taken and even taught numerous food safety courses. I knew the practices associated with food poisoning, and I had seen about all of them since we arrived. One safe beverage, however, is any type of soft drink bottled and sealed in a bottling plant. The bottles are sanitized and they are tightly sealed after they are filled. I was pretty happy to see some nice, safe Pepsi coming our way. Our host went over to a place in the shade and moved a canvas tarp. Under the tarp was a large chunk of green colored, frozen river water. After being broken into small chunks with a heavy hammer that had been taken out of the repair pit, the ice became a part of the Pepsi service. Green ice chunks were put into a glass, and the Pepsi poured over it. It took most of that week in Viet Nam for me to learn that I was not taking care of myself. My knowledge and skills were not feeding or sustaining me. The Lord wanted me to learn to trust Him, and He is a very thorough teacher.

Sunday morning came and the Americans had a time of prayer and worship together. Taking our group to any of the little underground churches would have drawn a lot of unwanted attention from government authorities. I came to realize how dangerous it was for the believers there to be seen with me. At the same time, I thought about how awful it would be if I was the cause of one of these precious people being jailed, or worse. After Sunday lunch, our team leader spoke with the lead pastor who hosted us. It had been decided that we would hold an evening service. Further, it had been decided that I was to be the guest speaker. How does a business man from America, prepare a sermon to minister to persecuted Vietnamese believers, and do it in just a couple of hours? Unlike pastors, businessmen do not always keep two or three messages prepared ahead in case the opportunity to preach arises. Businessmen can, however, devote time every morning to studying the Word of God and building a strong personal relationship with the God of that Word. Businessmen also should be decision makers, and able to look around and assess situations. They should understand who they are and what God is doing in their lives. When I looked at the Vietnamese believers and thought about who they were and who I was, Philippians 1:1-11 came quickly into my mind. As Paul expressed in this text, I was so thankful that God had brought me to Viet Nam to meet the believers there. I felt a strong bond of kinship with them. The grace which had encompassed their existence had also encompassed me. I looked at their persecution and hardship and all of my human reasoning said they had an impossible task. Like Paul in Philippians, I was confident that He who had begun the work in these Vietnamese believers would complete it. When church time arrived that evening, the Americans set up in one of our hotel rooms. The Vietnamese came one or two at a time with intervals carefully spaced between arrivals. Security was the word of the day, or at least in getting assembled. We opened in prayer and they began to sing praise and worship songs. I noticed that as this song service went on, it got louder. Our room was just a few feet away from a wooden fence, and right on the other side of that fence was the sidewalk and public street. I was certain we would see police storming in most any moment, but we did not! Being able to share the passage in Philippians was an unbelievably special experience for me. I cherish it to this day. While I am not a touchy feely kind of guy, there was, no doubt, a sense of love and a bond of unity that developed among us that evening. Romans 8:16 tells us that the Holy Spirit Himself bears witness with our spirit that we are children of God. I celebrate this realization. The believers in every country are my brothers and sisters in Christ. That is a wonderful truth, and a strong motivator to be a part of bearing their burdens however I can.

Time to say good-bye came too quickly. I knew that I would return there. In fact, I had known that Asia was going to hold a different place in my life from the minute I had arrived. I have returned a number of times to Viet Nam over the years. I not only took materials, but I taught pastors in underground seminaries. I have visited in homes, ridden on the river in their boats, and have preached in their churches. I have seen the country become much more open toward Christians. Our schedule this day, however, was to return to Bangkok, Thailand, overnight, and head for Nepal the next day. I had become comfortable in the Vietnamese environment, and I was, quite frankly, terrified about traveling into Nepal. Within twenty four hours I would, in fact, deplane in Nepal.

Much has changed in Nepal since the night that I first set foot there. At that time, international flights were parked on the tarmac, and passengers were required to descend a long steep stairway to the ground, before hiking to a small poorly lighted building. It was after dark when we arrived. As we entered the little terminal building, a virtual sea of humanity surrounded us. Many hands grabbed at our carry-on bags and many bodies thronged against us as we made our way to the luggage belt. Did I say luggage belt? What I meant was we went to the opening in the building where several porters were unloading bags from a hand cart. They unloaded the entire cargo hold of a 747 onto push carts, making trip after trip until all baggage had been brought into the terminal. We simply waited until we saw someone lift our bags up onto the platform, and then we squeezed through the crowd to retrieve them. All the while, people kept taking hold of our carry-ons or the checked bags we had, saying in broken English, "I carry your bag, sir. I carry your bag." These people looked, sounded and acted differently than any I had ever seen before. Sadly, most of my life, to this point, had been interacting only within the confines of western civilization. Viet Nam had been a little different than America, but the recent French and American military presence had westernized the country quite a bit. Nepal, in 1996, was all Asia all the time! Just as I had a perspective on what I believed they were doing, they also had a perspective. The westerners getting off of the plane were surely wealthy tourists who would tip a baggage porter the equivalent of a week's wages for helping with their bags.

Amid the confusion, the multitudes and my lack of understanding, I felt very uneasy about my surroundings. I would learn that the poverty of this nation, at the time, was so great that everyone was essentially in survival mode. Western decorum is meaningless to a father who has put his children to bed without feeding them anything that day. As I am writing this, strong emotions are flooding back. I had heard about great poverty, but I would spend a week in the midst of it, and would never be the same. John the Elder wrote in his epistle, I John 3:17: "But whosoever has this world's goods, and sees his brother in need, and shuts up his heart from him, how does the love of God abide in him?" If a Christ follower ever needs to test his spiritual temperature, he should spend time among very needy people and measure his emotions and his actions toward them.

Our western missionary host, who met us at the airport, loaded us into a van and took us to a modest hotel, right in the heart of the tourist district. Everything about the twenty or thirty block area was tourist hotels, shops or restaurants. People like me, who were overwhelmed by culture shock, could retreat into some semblance of familiarity, dining at European restaurants and visiting shops where proprietors learned English so they could sell tourists things. We ate a late supper and retired to our rooms for the night. My roommate and I soon learned that there was no heat in the room, and we piled on all of the clothing we could to keep ourselves warm enough to sleep through the night. January in Kathmandu can be incredibly cold.

We spent the next day getting to know our host and his international family. He was American, his wife Indian, and his children adopted from several countries. He had originally been a part of a three missionary team which had entered Nepal on student visas. The others had left due to interpersonal conflict and burnout. This missionary would also succumb to burnout within months after we visited. God used this man to introduce me to a Nepali pastor who is to this day one of the key partners in our ministry in Nepal. In turn, the Lord used me to confront this man about issues that had caused strife with his former coworkers. He was a huge mountain of a man, standing six feet six and weighing over three hundred pounds. He had the aggressive persona to match his looks, though he really didn't want to appear to be as intimidating as he was. As the missions committee chairman at my church for many years, I had talked with many missionaries about a host of issues. I was very much in my element, and if I had more time, I think we would have become very good friends. As it was, we crossed paths at the Lord's appointment, and never saw one another after that week together.

The next day, we drove out of Kathmandu into some small villages just north of the city. As we drove around the winding roads, we frequently called out to our host to stop so that we could take photos. Back in those days, cameras used film rather than electronic digits. I had twenty three rolls of film, each with a capacity of twenty four pictures. I would purchase a few more rolls of film before the trip ended. At one stop, our team was appalled to see young girls carrying heavy loads of rocks in baskets on their backs. They were constructing a new wall to surround a rice field. A man walked along beside them, without carrying anything, but barking out angry orders. Child labor was not unusual in Nepal, and girls were not seen as educable. From our western perspective, this was very abusive. One of our team members wanted to start a physical altercation with the man on the spot, but cooler heads prevailed. Our world is a cruel place. Christian values have shaped our thinking, but this man was a Hindu, and the Hindu world view was such that we all earn our fate in this life by what we did in our last life. He could not know what these low caste girls had done in their past lives to deserve such a demeaning position, but he could hope they would behave differently in this life to earn a better place in the next life.

As we rolled further along the road, I spotted a darling little girl, and asked the driver to stop. I used to carry lollipops or toys to give to children in the places where I traveled. I gave this little girl a plastic bead necklace and a lollipop. As I squatted interacting with this precious little girl, I saw the mother standing about twenty meters away, watching. She had a posture indicating a great uneasiness about seeing this foreigner there with her daughter. I prayed a blessing on this child, and returned to our van. I would later learn that thousands of little girls each year are taken from their families in Nepal and trafficked into the brothels in India. Little girls like this one were targeted for these purposes. Those little girls, who were spared being trafficked, often ended up being sold into slavery by their parents, who needed to feed the other children in their households. Nearly every child in Nepal had to contend with lack of food, lack of medical care, and difficulties that we cannot start to comprehend in America. The bleak outlook for children in Nepal would be one of the issues that our ministry would one day address.

We arrived at a house on the edge of a little village. Here we met a woman named Kanchi. She supported herself selling tea. No sooner had we sat down than she prepared tea for us. She picked up her cup of tea, covered her head with her shawl, and gave thanks to the Lord for her tea. Those of us who had already been sipping our tea were adequately ashamed that we had not been the example to her that she had been to us. It soon became apparent that our team of American Christians was not the one delivering a blessing that day. Kanchi began to tell us her story. Like so many Nepali women, Kanchi had married young to a man her father had chosen. She did a great deal of very hard work to help their family survive. One day, Kanchi became ill. None of her home remedies helped. The local medicine man exacted a fee, but his demonic incantations gave her no relief. Finally, her husband saw her as a liability rather than as an asset, and he sent her away. Kanchi boarded a bus and made the trip down to the city, to try to find a sister she had not seen or talked with for years. She hoped she could live her remaining few days with her sister. As Kanchi got off of the bus, she was approached by a woman who struck up a conversation. This woman was a Christian. In those days, Nepal's population was a little over twenty million, and there were fewer than a thousand known believers in the country. Kanchi was taken in and cared for by this Christian woman. There was no discernable reason why this woman would do this for Kanchi. In short, this woman was practicing the love of Christ. The woman began to pray for Kanchi, and strength began to return to Kanchi's body. After being miraculously healed by the God, to whom this Christian prayed, Kanchi wanted to know this God. She became a follower of Jesus, and returned home to her husband's house. Upon hearing this story, the husband and all of the family received Christ. I would learn over the years that many of the first believers in Nepal and India came to Christ after being healed through the prayers of the Christians. I would also learn that without the help of a professional pastor/church planter, these early believers would be drawn together and ultimately become a local church. Such is my conviction, that when God does a work, He doesn't need me, but He extends the privilege of being an observer and sometimes even a participant in the work.

The next day, I met an evangelist named Peter. While a member of the Gurkhas, a Nepali unit of the British Army, he had heard about Jesus and become a Christian. Upon leaving the British Army, he returned home, and wisely used his English language skills and his superb conditioning to become a trekking guide in the mountains of Nepal. For many years, he traveled all through the hillsides and became well known to the people of the villages who benefitted from the tourists he would bring there for trekking. As a natural outflowing of his new found faith, he shared Christ with these people in the remote villages. Many came to Christ over the years. Going against all western ministry philosophy, which requires a seminary trained church planter, the Christ followers in these remote villages were drawn together by the Holy Spirit, and churches began to form. This became a very profound notion as I would later move into a late in life missionary career. I met absolutely no preconceived conditional requirement for a western church planter, but I could do a number of things to help strengthen these precious churches that God was building. Since that time in Nepal, I have visited hundreds of churches that no western missionary could call his own. I have a strong conviction that the only church planter that exists is the Holy Spirit. He does allow us to be a small part from time to time, but He doesn't need our help, nor is He obliged to meet our guidelines.

We visited the church of Pastor M. He would become one of the founding partners of Allow The Children, seven years later. One had to be impressed with Pastor M and his church family. In addition to the main church, daughter churches and cell groups were now meeting in seventeen other locations in Nepal. Remember that at this time, there were very few Christians in Nepal, so Pastor M was extremely influential in shaping the present day landscape of Nepal's Christian community. A very humble man, this pastor had seen God work in many marvelous ways. At the time, any one participating in the conversion of a Hindu to Christianity risked being jailed for six years. This man had already baptized hundreds. He would not call upon any of his assistants or evangelists to put themselves at risk. If anyone was going to go to jail, it was going to be him. I marveled at how pure this man's faith was and how obedient he was to the commands of our Lord. Without the trappings of western churches, he simply moved forward with church as it was meant to be, and God blessed it.

A part of our mission to Nepal was to contact some Tibetan believers with whom we might come along side and encourage. We met a number of interesting Tibetans, but none who followed Christ. I was impressed how these refugees from Tibet had built a business infrastructure to provide economically for other refugees who would follow. They had fled their homeland with only the clothes on their backs. Tibetans had no real rights in Nepal, and they were even looked down upon as people to be avoided. We would minister among the Tibetans in later years and discover just how resistant to the Gospel they were.

Our time in Nepal was ending, and I was splitting off from the team to join my wife at the Laos/Thai border. The team would go to India and then on to Cambodia. I would later minister in both of these countries on several trips, as God taught me how to serve Him in places way out of my comfort zone. I watched as my taxi driver and his helper struggled to get my large luggage into the back of the taxi. In those days, people were allowed to put seventy-five pounds in a suitcase, and mine was every bit of that. On the drive to the airport, the helper, who could speak a little English, asked me the standard question that would be asked of a tourist who was leaving: "What did you like best about your visit to Nepal?" I heard strange words coming out of my mouth: "I like the Nepali people." Only a week earlier I had been very uneasy standing among the Nepali people who were all around me at the airport and in the crowded streets and shops. Now, I had a love that had cropped up in my heart for a people who were very strange to me. Indeed, the feelings in my heart were more foreign to me than the people to which they were directed. I knew that I would return to Nepal. There was not a good administrative reason to do so, but I was certain that I would. God had firmly established Nepal as a place of blessing for me, and transformed my heart attitude as only the Almighty can do.

During the week we had been in Nepal, the government had opened their new international airport. It was not huge, but it was much larger than the little terminal at which we had arrived. As I sat in the airport boarding lounge, I thought about the trip to Nepal. So much was spinning around in my head as I sat waiting. I could not, at the time, connect the dots. My heritage passed on to me by my mother, father, and grandparents, was that of a people who were very poor, living in a remote mountainous region. It was also that of a people who had missionaries come to share Christ, and to help them stem the endless cycle of poverty which had prevailed in their region for two centuries. As the only son of my mother, and only grandson of my grandmother, I had been the focus of their hope that one day I might be a "pastor" which to them was a man who had come to their area as an outside missionary.

I did not take this trip to become a missionary. My intent was to increase my knowledge base to be able to better help my church and its existing missionaries. I had, indeed, greatly increased my knowledge base over the past two weeks, but I also increased my experience base as well. Most particularly, I had experienced God in ways that I had never thought I would. I had walked paths of faith that I had never walked before. I had my heart broken in ways it had never been broken before. More importantly, however, I found God using me to answer the cries of people who lived on the other side of the world from me. I saw the focus of several years of my own prayers come to life, as I walked among the unreached, the fatherless, the poor and the persecuted. These were no longer nameless, faceless entities for which I entreated God's help. These were now real people that I knew, and God had used me to answer their prayers. He had also used the Nepali people to answer my prayers!

I was treated to Sprite and peanuts by the airline, and finally ushered aboard the Thai Air flight to Bangkok. I looked forward to being back together with Sue. When I am apart from her, I feel like the best part of me is missing. I wanted to take Sue to Nepal. I would do so two years later.

When the plane landed in Bangkok, I was met by our American contact on the ground. As we walked to his car in the parking lot, he laid out my agenda for the next day. I would depart from the domestic airport at daylight. I would fly into a tiny airport, where I would be met by a Thai man and driven two hours to the village by the river where Sue and the medical team were. He then took a baseball cap off of his head and put it on mine. This would be how the Thai man knew he had the right person to transport. Ordinarily I would have quickly asked, "How will I know that he is the right Thai man to get in the truck with?" For some reason, my planning had given way to my trusting, and I was content.

At daylight, I boarded the small plane and made the short flight. With cap firmly in place, I deplaned and walked into the tiny terminal. It was packed with people, all but one of which was Thai. As the lone foreigner, I really stood out. Two teen-age Thai girls approached me. In slow, deliberate and well-spaced words, one of the girls asked, "You are Michael?" They knew only a few words of English. I knew even less Thai. They led me to an Asian manufactured double cab pickup truck. My bags were put in the back, the girls were seated in the rear seats of the cab, and I sat in the front passenger's seat by the driver. The driver spoke no English, and had brought the two Thai girls along to translate. The girl who was considered the English speaker, from time to time would ask me some three or four word questions. For one extended period, the two girls jabbered away with each other, as teen-age girls worldwide do. I had no idea what they were saying. The driver entered their discussion, and the tone became more serious. Finally, the spokes-girl leaned forward and in her best English, asked me, "How do we know you are Michael?" I chuckled a bit at the potential irony of this, and at the sweetness and sincerity in her voice. I then took off the cap and waved it. This was the sign for which she had been looking.

At long last, after traveling through countless villages and farmlands, we arrived at a house situated in sight of the river bank. The Mekong and its tributaries are very important rivers in Southeast Asia. The lead pastor and his wife, a Thai couple with American citizenship, had departed a few weeks earlier for America. I also learned that the team which included Sue had crossed the river and were visiting a hospital in Laos. When I walked into the door, the church which met in this house was in the closing part of their morning Sunday school. I was greeted warmly by the assistant pastor, an energetic young Thai man. As I was sitting down, he then announced to the group in both Thai and English, "Michael is the husband of Susan. He has come to be with us and will preach the message at morning service which will begin immediately following Sunday school." Let me repeat an important point that I made earlier. I was a businessman, and businessmen do not keep spare sermons ready to preach at a moment's notice. God had given me a message a few hours before it was to be preached in Vietnam. Could He do the same within a few minutes here in Thailand? As the singing of the church service began, my eyes looked out through the window, and I saw the large trees that grew along the river bank. Immediately, the Lord brought Psalm 1 to my mind. This was a Psalm I had memorized. I had meditated upon this Psalm, and actually taught it in devotional times. Of course I had no notes or outline, but I knew this would be what I would preach. The metaphor of the psalm is that those who trust in the Lord will be like the fruitful trees which are planted by the water. Their roots go deep to the water, and they never are dried up. Going verse by verse, I delivered one of the best messages of my life. No, I did not intend to change careers and become a pastor. I did, however, see much more to bolster my conviction that great men of God are simply men who join God in what He is doing, and give Him the full credit for the success.

Sue and the team returned from Laos, and resumed medical clinics. They would go to one village in the morning and another in the evening. The clinics were held out of doors, and whole villages would come to see the doctors and nurses. Each clinic had been pre-approved by the village chief, and he and his family were usually the first patients to be seen. Even those who had nothing wrong would get in line to see the medical people. When using the term "medical worker" and my name, it is always improper to use them in the same sentence unless a big *not* is included. I married a nurse, and she filled a glaring weakness in my skill set. So, what would a non- medical person do in a week of medical clinics? The clinics were being held to open up new villages to the Gospel. Each person who saw the doctor, left with whatever medicine he or she needed, and with a packet of literature. Pills had to be counted out and put into sandwich bags for the patients. Literature needed to be collated into distributable packets. These were time-consuming tasks but needed to be done. I know how to count. I know how to collate literature, or at least I thought I did. The Lord was going to give me a lesson in culture that would greatly enhance my ability to teach in Asia. All of us Americans who have ever collated documents of any kind have used a tried and true method for years. We clear off a space on the conference table and take page one and "deal out" a dozen of them face down. We then put a page two on top of the page one, a page three on page two, and so forth, until we have a dozen completed packets. As I started to do this, I noticed that the teen girls, who seemed to have been tasked with making sure the foreigner was doing okay, were both looking at me. They very respectfully showed me how I should be assembling a packet. Their method was to assemble one complete packet, then another complete packet, and so on. While they did not express anything negative, they certainly marveled that I was not schooled on how to collate a simple packet of materials. I would study and learn that only our western minds think in assembly line fashion. The girls were building a complete package, before moving on to build another one. I was breaking down a pile of page ones into individual components and arranging them into a manageable array. This difference isn't as critical to document collation as it is to Bible teaching. When we listen to our western pastor, he is analyzing or breaking down the text from his Bible. Asian minds think in terms of the whole. Breaking things down into small components goes against the way they do things. When I preach in Asia, I don't take a Bible story and break it down for the Asians. They deal with the story as a whole quite nicely. This is especially true in remote villages, where most people don't read. Their culture and history have been passed down orally, and their lives are very much a part of the whole village. Americans are products of an individualistic culture, focusing on me and my rather than "our."

As we departed from our village on the border, we were all huddled together in the back of the pickup truck, amongst the luggage. Remarkably, the hot climate we had experienced all week was totally absent on this pre-dawn ride, and our lack of warm clothing proved to be unfortunate. (We did survive, however, and boarded the short flight back to Bangkok.) The next day, we left for home. I really don't have much memory of that flight. I knew that my perspective on the world, on missions, and on my life in general was changed. I knew I would return some day, and I did.

We Didn't Come This Far to Turn Back

So, what do you do when the Lord totally rocks your world? How do you restore normalcy to your thought patterns which have just been put through a high speed blender? Where do you navigate when your ship has just been cut loose from its moorings and pushed out to sea? Sue and I were struck by how God had suited our appointments in Asia with people who needed the ministry which He had equipped us to do. We began talking about a return to Asia as soon as we got home. Responsibilities, commitments, and the tyranny of the mundane soon engulfed us. It would be two years before we would return, but return we would.

At this point in my life, I was not a missionary. I was a businessman, with daily responsibilities. I was the chairman of the missions committee of a very missions-minded church. I was the father of five children, three of whom still lived at home, and would one by one be moving into their college years. Sue and I stayed in the Asia loop by joining the Board of Directors of the organization which had sponsored our first trip to Asia.

My dad had purchased several burial plots in a new cemetery which was located a short distance from his house. My grandfather had been laid to rest, and a headstone for him and my grandmother's future grave next to his had been installed. My mother and grandmother were at peace with his departure from this life. His time after the stroke had been frustrating and unhappy. We all believed that he was now in a much better place, experiencing the fullness of joy only his Savior could give. I would go to this grave a number of times over the next fifteen years, taking my mother to put flowers on it around different holidays.

Cemeteries, by their very nature, facilitate our walking away from the loved ones we leave there, and moving forward with the rest of the time we have in our own lives. We actually don't lose our loved ones, because we retain the memories of their lives and what they had meant to us. My grandfather was, of course, my mother's step-father. I never knew my biological grandfather. The grandfather I did know was humble, kind, generous and hard working. He kept tools and seemed to be able to fix anything. He knew how to grow things in the ground, because he had been a farmer for many years. He followed my mother north, and had worked in Cleveland for a number of years. He had retired with a pension from the automaker that had employed him. He worked in the business that my dad and I ran, doing various maintenance tasks. He also grew a garden at my parents' home. He was ever in motion doing something, but never in a hurry. I had a great love and respect for this man. He had not been given the luxury of finishing school. Instead, he had to quit school to help on the farm. He had dealt with poverty and hardship, and had lived a simple life. Even though he was now out of the poverty, he still led a simple life. He did not worship at the altar of materialism. He had what was needed, and that was enough. He and my grandmother would find people who had great needs, and help them.

I remember a woman who lived in the next apartment from them in Cleveland. This woman, a recent immigrant to the United States, gave birth to a son, only to have her husband leave her and never return. She was not employed at the time, and lacked the money to buy food or clothing for herself or her baby. She lost her apartment. My grandparents opened their home. They let her have the spare bedroom, and she stayed with them for several months, until she found work and got on her feet again. They maintained a relationship with the woman and son even after they had moved away from each other. My grandparents were not wealthy, but they were willing to extend a hand to a woman with a fatherless child. This, of course, had been my grandmother's plight many years before. When she remarried-to my grandfather- he, in turn, was helping a woman with a fatherless child. The character of my grandfather imprinted itself on my life quite a bit more than I had realized. I am thankful that the Lord put him into my life.

Beginning in 1986, I started reading through the Bible once a year. Actually, it takes me a little more than nine months to read totally through the Bible during my morning quiet time. I also started keeping a journal of the insights I received from God's Word each day. Along with this, I developed a prayer list which was adjusted both by life events, and by spiritual truths which I learned from my Bible study. Some of these prayer requests were for people groups who were unreached by the Gospel. Some were for people with certain circumstances like poverty or persecution. Early on, I added a generic prayer for "fatherless children." I put this on the list because of scriptures which command us to minister to the widow and the fatherless. I didn't consciously think about it at the time, but my heart had been touched by my mother and my grandparents who had lived this experience in the most personal of ways. An important lesson we can learn was summed up by a preacher I heard. "If God commands you to dig a well in the desert, when you finish, look around for the person that God is sending to you for a drink." Yes, God does let us quench our thirst, but He uses our circumstances, or interaction with His Word, and our prayer lives to move us to *ministry*. After having prayed for fatherless children for some time, I had an experience which was new and frightening to me. Seemingly out of the blue, I felt an unbelievably strong prompting in my heart to give a specific sum of money to a widow in our church, who had two children. I had to do this, but felt it better to do it anonymously through an intermediary. I put the exact amount I felt led to give into an envelope, and gave it to our associate pastor. I asked him to give it to the widow, but to keep my name totally out of it. I was giving this money not to receive thanks, but as a privilege. My status as a businessman provided enough that I was neither hurting my own family nor even sacrificing. I was simply obeying what I believed was a prompting from God. I was given a note a couple of weeks later by the pastor who had delivered the gift. The note addressed to "The Person who gave us the gift," emotionally shared how the family had been facing financial hardships and was not able to exchange gifts at Christmas. The money that I had given would greatly lessen their burden and help bring a blessed time at Christmas. From an investment standpoint, I couldn't have done better. From a spiritual standpoint, I had prayed in principle for fatherless children, and the Lord now tested my heart to see how sincere my prayers were. Actually, the Lord knew how sincere my prayers were. He was showing me that He could use me if I was willing to take a step of faith.

My grandmother was now dependent upon family to take her places and to make sure she had everything she needed. My mother took the lead in this and went to my grandmother's house nearly every day. I fell into a regular routine of stopping by on Saturdays when I was in town, just to visit with her. I learned a lot during these visits. It was during these times when bits of family history that I didn't know would come up. I came to realize just how much poverty and hardship she and most of my relatives had endured over the years. I also continued to see her amazing faith on display. From my earliest memories of Nanny, when she experienced something that seemed unjust or observed something too difficult for her to understand, she would tell me, "Mike, we just have to trust the good Lord!" She did trust the good Lord with all of her heart. When frustrations, sorrows, or problems arose, she would hold a prayer meeting on the spot with me or whoever else might be there. She would say, "Let's ask the Good Lord to help us." Despite all of the tribulations she had been through in her lifetime, she never wavered from her sense of the goodness of God. All that I learned from this dear lady would drop neatly into place as God's purposes for my life were rolled out before me. I did have to trust the good Lord, and I had to go to Him in prayer to plead for His help many times.

The Changes of a Called Life

The time frame from early 1996 to early 2003 was a time of major transition for Sue and me. In April of 1998, I made my return to Nepal, along with Sue and a team of four others. Sue and another team member who was a nurse held a medical clinic in a Tibetan refugee village. I did some teaching and met a number of Nepali pastors. Perhaps the highlight of the trip, however, was our time visiting a children's home. The children were led in prayer, worship, and Bible study every morning and every evening. Coming from remote villages or refugee camps, most of these children had been either orphaned or abandoned by parents who could no longer feed them. Of even greater significance was the fact that none of them had ever heard the name of Jesus before coming to this children's home. Here was a form of evangelism wrapped up in tremendous good works, which was being done by locals. We were able, at this time, to enter into a relationship with this children's home that would last for ten years, and allow us to participate in changing the lives of many children. We would also tuck this methodology away in our minds, to be brought out in many other localities in the future. In addition to the ministry in Nepal, we also traveled to Cambodia, where we participated in similar ministry work. During one medical clinic, Sue worked in heat of 120 degrees. Her recognition of the perilous dehydration situation of a baby enabled us to buy formula for this baby and literally save its life. God was continuing to show us that there were needs which we could meet in many different places.

The business that my dad and I operated was thriving. That was both a good thing and a problem. Following our return trip to Asia, both Sue and I felt that we were being moved to take a major step in the direction of mission work. The insanity of this idea was not lost on me. Working as a businessman, I could, and did, help a number of missionaries financially. My work with the church missions committee was productive. I served on the Board of Directors of a mission agency. Sue was similarly active in our church. There was no reason to interrupt the good work that we had been doing. The classic struggle for so many people who are called into a new ministry is to be willing to leave what is very good, to pursue what one believes is God's best. I privately put this issue before the Lord. My nature is to avoid adventure and cautiously stay within a well-defined environment which I can control. Sue has no such reluctance. She was ready to go and just waiting on the Lord to move in my life. I privately asked the Lord to enable us within five years to depart the business world, and be able to follow Him anywhere in the world that He would lead. Looking back, this was somewhat of a proverbial fleece, to see if God was indeed calling us out of what was a blessed and comfortable life, into the unknown. I thought in terms of a very controlled five-year plan to make this happen. Before 1998 ended, God had brought a buyer out of nowhere, to buy the business that my dad and I had been operating. We were able to invest proceeds into rental real estate which could be managed by a local property management company. A further answer came in April 1999, when the Lord moved on our church to commission us as "At Large" missionaries, who would minister in whatever countries the Lord would open up before us.

The world is a big place, but we certainly went into a lot of it over the four years following our commissioning. We traveled into Russia, China, Cambodia, Viet Nam, Laos, Cambodia, Cuba, Mexico, India, and, of course, Nepal. We taught church leaders. We encouraged Christ followers who were experiencing persecution. We took Bibles to those who had none. We provided medical help to those who had no doctor. We fed the poor, the fatherless, and the widow. More importantly, however, we were students in God's schoolhouse, learning how to minister effectively in these cross-cultural scenarios. God was opening the world before us, and we loved every square foot of it. We began to realize, however, that we needed to begin to focus on a smaller territory, and go deeper. God used this time to help us build relationships with men and women who are now our trusted ministry partners, and quite frankly, who we consider as our family.

God was taking us through a number of other life changes as well. My grandmother became unable to live by herself, so she moved in with my mother. This worked for a few years, but ultimately, a seventy-something woman caring for a ninety-something person, eventually wears down the caregiver. My grandmother experienced a series of falls, and required more care than my mother could give her. With great tears flowing down my mother's cheeks, she allowed my grandmother to be moved into an assisted living facility. This worked out better than we could have imagined. Nanny had more company than she could handle. She moved into a room with one of her close friends, and this was just a wonderful situation. My mother was there in person many times each week, and on the phone with her on the days she couldn't come. I lived very near the assisted living facility, so I established a regular visiting schedule. It was still sad to acknowledge that this was her home, but it really did provide the best of all worlds for all involved.

Meanwhile, Sue and I were becoming empty nesters. The rest of our children were finishing high school, going off to college and establishing independent lives of their own. Early on when we traveled out of the country, we would have one of the teachers from our Christian high school come and stay with our teen-age children. Now, we no longer needed this kind of arrangement. We were traveling out of country three or four times each year. We could not shake a sense of restlessness, though, about a point of focus and a need to go deeper. We were enjoying traveling and ministering in numerous places. God had provided investments from our business sale that now financially supported us. We had a connection with an agency by way of our directorship on its board, but we could see that agency going in one direction, and God was pulling us in another direction. In 2001, the U.S. went through the September 11 attacks. This not only changed the American psyche forever, it changed the travel industry forever. Several airlines were forced to merge with other airlines because of the financial damage. Flights that we had previously made into our ministry countries were no longer in existence. Cheap fares to Asia were history. We were exhorted to cancel the ministry trips we had scheduled for October of 2001, a mere month after the attacks, and only a couple of weeks after airline service had been restarted. We found ourselves not even considering cancelations. Our trust in God had matured beyond what even we had realized. If He was leading us to Asia, He would take us there and back at His good pleasure. We boarded the nearly empty flights, and made our trips. In Asia, our partners pleaded with us to stay there because America was very dangerous for us. A bond of love had developed between us and our partners, and they genuinely wanted to see us remain safe.

In 2002, we parted company with the agency with which we had been associated. Looking back, this was a Paul and Barnabus situation. Their understanding of God's will and our understanding of it were irreconcilable. We briefly looked at associating with another agency, but after a week of talks and visiting with them, it became clear that this was not where we belonged. The year 2002 also had a life altering set of circumstances for Sue. Her eighty-two-year-old father had to go onto dialysis. Sue had to drive him across town for his regular appointments. She was grounded from international travel from mid-year until her father passed away the following year. The next time Sue would travel, our ministry focus would be radically changed.

As I looked at my planning calendar, I had two trips scheduled for 2003. Both were largely to explore new ministry opportunities. Sue and I both felt like God had something for us that He would reveal to us in His time. I was excited as my March departure date arrived. I flew into Izmir, Turkey to join over three-hundred fifty people who were interested in ministering among Muslims. Ever since the September eleventh attacks, the buzz among frontier missionaries was about showing God's love to the people who so many Americans now hated. Admission to this meeting was by invitation only, and I had to submit recommendations from pastors and others who could vouch for me, because of the sensitive nature of the meeting topic. I really enjoyed the time of fellowship, prayer, and worship among the people at this meeting. The breakout groups were very informative, and I seemed to accomplish most of what I had hoped to accomplish. By all human standards, my time at the week-long conference was a great success. I had developed several key ministry contacts that seemed to be a perfect fit for Sue and me. One involved an orphanage in Chechnya. Sue and I had ministered to some Chechnyan widows when we had visited Russia three years earlier. We knew a little about their plight. Ministering to orphans was something we had experienced in several Asian countries. Other open doors were for partnering with ministries in a variety of Middle Eastern countries. I left with a strong sense that we could plug in to one of these ministries and have a positive impact. I was waiting for that special wave of peace and joy which engulfs us so often when we have come face to face with the people God has brought us to serve. The problem was, it just wasn't there. None of these would be our special place of blessing.

My next scheduled trip was to Nepal in May. A meeting of people ministering among the Tibetan Buddhists was being held. This, also, was an invitation only meeting. Unlike the meeting in Turkey, this meeting, by all human standards, was a total failure for me. Because of a national strike, most of the hands-on ministry people could not travel to the city where we were meeting. Only a small group of American agency personnel was in attendance, and there were absolutely no new contacts for me to make. I had scheduled an extra week and a half to be in Nepal, to visit the people I had ministered among for several years. I really thought that this would be my last trip there. I presumed that God would connect us with the right ministry in the Middle East and we would focus our work there. One of the many bad habits I have is presuming upon God. From my perspective, however, everything seemed to be pointing to the Middle East. God had taken me to Turkey. He had connected me with ministries there which seemed a good fit for us, and I could easily see us working with these ministries. In a conversation with one of the agency representatives who was at the small meeting in Nepal, the topic of ministry among Muslims came up. He made the observation that many American agencies were now flooding into the Muslim areas, but practically no one was working in Hindu and Buddhist areas. I filed this away in my memory bank, but never really thought about it until months later.

I met with a mother and her baby whom I had known from previous trips to Nepal. Sue had led this woman to Christ, and had named the baby for her. Sadly, this woman's husband had abandoned her, and she was living hand-to-mouth. Sue and I were helping her and I met her at a restaurant to give her some funds I had brought for that purpose. I bought her a meal and a Coke, which is a big treat for most Nepalis, and made sure that the baby had nourishment as well. When I called for my check, the restaurant manager said he did not want me to pay, because he had observed the kindness and respect which I had shown this Nepali lady and her baby. I actually cared a lot for them, and had not really gone out of my way to treat them specially. The restaurant manager was seeing something that my eyes were not fully open to yet. This would come soon.

I had invited a pastor to come visit me at my hotel. He could get around the city much easier than I could. I considered this man a dear friend as well as a pastor whom I greatly respected in Nepal. When he arrived, he had his assistant pastor with him. We sat and chatted for a while. Before leaving for Nepal, a man at my church had given me a one hundred dollar bill to take along with me. He had said, "God will show you who you should give this to." I still had it, and suddenly, I got a strong prompting in my heart to give the hundred dollar bill to this pastor. I waited for a pause in the conversation, before I pulled out the money and put it into the pastor's hand. I told him that a Christian man in America had told me to give this to the one that God showed me, and that God was prompting me to give it to him. Things were quiet for a moment, before the pastor held up the hundred dollar bill and said, "We will give thanks to the Lord for this gift." Just as if he was saying grace over a meal, the pastor thanked God for this gift. The pastor then related a story to me that still sends chills up and down my spine. The assistant pastor with him had last week taken into his home, four little girls who had been living on the streets. This man could barely feed his own family, and really did not know how he could feed four more hungry children. He had been in prayer, asking God to help. I brought the help, twelve-thousand miles around the globe, as an answer to his prayer. At this point, I was rejoicing in my heart to have been the one God used to bring this answer to prayer. I understood now, that God had a purpose other than a meeting when He brought me to Nepal, but, my understanding was only partial at this point.

The senior pastor shared with me that many members of his church were too poor to feed, provide clothing, or even get needed medical care for their children. He said, "If we could help these parents, our church would grow." He wasn't through there, however. He then looked at me and said, "Can you help us to help our children?"

I am seldom at a loss for words, but this tied my tongue. I finally answered, "I don't know if I can help you help your children. When I get home, I will pray. You be in prayer that God would give me the answer." We parted that evening with a sense of unfinished business. I knew this man to be one who did not shrink from challenges. My long range planning brain was already counting the cost and looking at how huge a task this really would be. What is huge to me is actually quite small to the Lord.

The next day I went to meet with a pastor that I had met on my first trip into Nepal. Over the years I had always visited him while I was in Nepal, but I never really had any ministry partnership with him. I marveled at the size of this church, and at the amazing evangelistic and church planting outreach it had built over the entire country. As we talked, the topic of our conversation went to the adversity that the evangelists were enduring. These men must travel two or three days back into remote villages. While they were away, they could not get any day labor jobs to earn income. Because of this, their families suffered. Children were prevented from going to school due to lack of funds. Food was often not available. This pastor then laid out an idea for me to consider. If someone would provide only a few dollars a month to help the children, the families would be stronger, and the evangelists more able to make their forays into the remote villages. Then he transposed the idea into a question: "Can you help us help these children?" I already had an answer to this question: "I don't know if I can help you help your children. When I get home, I will pray. You be in prayer that God would give me the answer."

One of my last stops of the trip was at a children's home we had visited many times and grown to love. We had actually procured a little funding for this children's home in the past, and I was carrying a small amount to give to them. The house parents were very thankful. They had forgone a birthday celebration they held every year for the children because they lacked funds. They shared that they were currently supported at only half of what it took to run the home. Then a rather familiar sounding question came," Can you help us help these children?" I had the same answer: "I don't know if I can help you help your children. When I get home, I will pray. You be in prayer that God would give me the answer."

As I made the long flight home, my mind raced trying to get a handle on what had taken place the past few weeks. I had just had my burning bush experience. God had made it abundantly clear that He wanted me to move into the ministry, and He had just used three different Nepalis to cast the vision for me. While this sounds simple, my brain kept generating all the reasons why it would not work. At the same time, I was mapping out what this would resemble. What type of structure would we need to put in place? How much time would it take? What would it cost? I supposed that when I laid this out in front of Sue, we would kick it around for a couple of hours, then think it over and pray about it for a few months, while researching all of the details before returning to Nepal to discuss it again with the pastors there. *I* wanted to make this happen, so at the first opportunity I had when I got home, I sat down with Sue. I laid out the vision that had been cast by the Nepali pastors, and was getting ready to launch into all the reasons that I thought this was a good idea, when Sue tersely replied, "Okay. Let's do it." Thank-you Lord for my wonderful wife Sue!

Where God Guides, God Provides

The next few weeks were full of testing of our will to follow God in these matters. It was also a time of sadness mixed with joy. Sue's father was at a healthcare crisis point. He had his ongoing kidney problems, and now we learned that he had lung cancer, and some heart issues. He could not tolerate chemo therapy for his cancer because of his kidney problems. He had taken all of the radiation treatments allowed, and now was left to wait for the cancer to run its course. Sue and her dad made the rounds, setting everything in order. They even arranged the funeral that would come all too soon. We had serious concerns that he had not given his life to Christ. His death was eminent, and both Sue and her mother urged him to receive Christ. Finally, as he lay in the hospital only a couple of days from his death, he looked at Sue's mother and said, "I guess it is time that I give my life to Jesus." He did just that. While we were very happy for this, we realized how rare it was for someone to make such a decision that late in his life. We laid Sue's father to rest the third week of May of that year.

During the last few weeks that Sue spent with her father, I was talking with our church leaders and our lawyer about what sort of structure was needed for us to be able to receive gifts, give tax credit to donors, and pass these funds along to our partners in Nepal. Sue and I had decided to receive general contributions, and child sponsorship funding for specific children we would bring into the program. My first choice was to work through our church. I wrongly thought that officials there would be very eager to be a part of the ministry we were launching. They were not. We didn't get a flat rejection, but we did get a deafening silence on our request.

It was clear that they did not oppose us, but were not interested in being a part of what we were doing, for their own undisclosed reasons. It was time to look elsewhere. My father had a charitable foundation that he had set up. I inquired of the tax experts about working through this foundation, but was told that it was not structured to do what we wanted to do. Our lawyer then broke the bad news to me. We would need to set up a not for profit corporation. Once that was completed, we would need to submit an application to the IRS for 501(c)3 status in order to receive tax deductible gifts. According to the attorney, who had done this procedure a number of times, we would submit the application, which was quite a long form. After about six months, the IRS would send back a letter asking us to submit specific changes. We would submit those, and hopefully, within the next six months, we would receive approval.

Since the journey of a thousand miles must begin with the first step, we needed to establish an organization, before we could move toward IRS approval of that organization. From the verse in Mark 10:14 came the name of our new organization. In the King James Version of the Bible, this verse quotes Christ as commanding His disciples, "Suffer the little children to come unto me, and forbid them not: for of such is the kingdom of God." Our modern day English uses the word "suffer" to mean something quite different, so we paraphrased suffer as "allow" to form the name of our organization. I used a model for incorporation that the State Corporation Commission had posted on line, to create Articles of Incorporation. I submitted them at the end of May, and on June 3, 2003, Allow The Children, Inc. received its registration as a Virginia not for profit corporation. I had only been home from Nepal two weeks, and step one was completed.

Step two, however, was the 501(c)3 approval, and that lay on the to do list of the lawyer. After a couple of weeks, I followed up to see how it was coming along. It had not actually left his in basket. He hadn't done anything to move the project forward. I decided to go on line to see just what would be needed to complete this application form. It was every bit as scary as it had been described to be. It was forty two pages long, and had detailed questions about the organizations purposes, its projected finances, and its methodology for raising and distributing funds. It was very much like a business plan for a charitable organization. It occurred to me that in order for the attorney to do this form, he was going to have to ask me all of these questions, so I began answering them. Over the next week I finished the full forty two pages. I then felt the desire to just submit what I had filled in. My reasons were manifold. The lawyer would charge me three thousand dollars to file this. I could do it for the hundred dollar filing fee charged by the government. The IRS would send back the required corrections, so I really didn't need to worry that I wasn't a lawyer and didn't know anything at all about registering a charitable organization. I also trusted God that if He really wanted this to happen, He could work it out- in spite of my ignorance. I put the application in the mail, and made a mental note that since this was late June, I would probably hear something by the end of the calendar year.

Looking back now, it is easy to see that God was working His plan not only through me, but through my wife. The Lord created me to wade through boring administrative issues, but He created Sue to march right to the front lines and work with people in a hands-on fashion. Sue scheduled her first international trip in over a year. She departed in late August to meet with the partners I had spoken with in May. She would tell them our plan, and let them know that we could start supporting a limited number of children, but that we would have to wait until we got our government approval before we could really take on a meaningful number of children. The small group of children turned out to be forty-five from the three different partners. One thing became abundantly clear; when you are face to face with a child who does not get to eat most days of the week, it is hard to tell him, "God bless you. If I can get a sponsor, I will send money to feed you."

We had a small amount of committed funds from some individuals who didn't need tax receipts. We also were personally involved. Sue was able to leave some funds that would ensure that these children ate for the next few months. Meanwhile, as August turned over to September, I got an envelope from the IRS. It was a standard business size envelope, and was very thin. My first thought was that this would be a letter acknowledging that they had received our application. As a veteran of college and graduate school applications, I was prone to think that good news came in a very thick envelope, and acknowledgments and rejections came in thin envelopes. I opened the letter, and began to read. It began with the standard heading which included our name, Allow The Children, Inc., and our EIN number which had been assigned. Then the body of the letter began. "Allow The Children has been approved for its status as a registered organization under section 501(c)3 of the IRS codes." I was totally stunned. What very good lawyers had said could not be done, had just been done. It had been done in a way that gave credit to God alone. The answer to our prayers and our stepping out in faith had been met by the power of the Almighty. Allow The Children was now fully registered, and prepared to receive donations. Sue always has greater faith than I, and I am not really sure she ever grasped how big an issue it was that we received this approval. Instead, she was focused on the next issue: How were we going to feed those forty-five children?

We had formed a very small Board of Directors for Allow The Children. At the time of our founding in June, we only had Sue, our Treasurer Doug, and me as the officers and directors of Allow The Children. Doug has been our friend for many years, and has been Treasurer of our church for a long time. He is very capable as a financial officer. More importantly, Doug is a man of great integrity. People who might donate to Allow The Children would know that we had a man like Doug as our Treasurer, and everything would be done decently and in order. We added Jean to our board next. Sue was taken aback, at first that I would want to appoint a woman to this position. Coming from a conservative church, we didn't see women serving in such leadership roles. I reminded Sue of what a capable leader Jean had been in the children's ministries for so many years, and how she was highly respected by everyone. Sue was very happy to put Jean on the board, but just a bit shocked that she was one of my first choices. We added our pastor and a couple of businessmen to the board. I laid out a five-year plan, which I thought was very bold and aggressive. We would grow to sponsor two hundred children by the end of the fifth year. We would train several church leaders and help establish some programs for our partner churches. I would soon be reminded that I was on God's five year plan and not mine. We would ultimately blow through my five year goals in fourteen months, but I am getting ahead of the story.

We traveled together to Nepal in November, taking our pastor and his wife with us. We wanted them to see firsthand that God was doing a great work in Nepal. We visited the children's home and added to our sponsorship program a few more children who had just been taken into the home. We visited the pastors who had established programs, and also found a need for a few more children to be sponsored. We were now beyond the scope of our resources to support all of these children. The next day, I came down with the twenty-four hour bug that sidelines foreign travelers all over the world. The plan was to visit a pastor who we knew that had a tiny church in a very poor area of the city. Sue took our pastor and his wife to visit, but I stayed in my room, barely able to get out of bed. When Sue returned that evening, I had started to recover a bit. She related a very sobering tale of thirteen orphan children who were living in the tiny church building. A few months earlier, a mudslide had taken out several villages and these thirteen children had lost their families. The pastor of this small church, who did regular evangelistic trips into this area, had brought these children to live at his church. Sue was very touched by their plight, but we had already gone over the limit of what we could support. The next day, I was back to normal, and my curiosity got the better of me. I caught a ride out to this little church. We were in the cold season, and Sue had left enough money to buy coats and shoes for the children, who had lost everything. As I looked at these children and spoke with the pastor, I found my mouth making a commitment that I knew was going to buy me a stern scolding from Sue. I told this pastor that he should pray and I would pray that God would give us sponsors for these children.

This was the only time in the history of Allow The Children that I stepped in front of Sue to make a child sponsorship decision. She is the Director of that ministry and she runs it very well. A good administrator lets his more capable people do their job and he stays out of their way! I heard a lot about this decision when I returned to our hotel, and repeatedly on our thirty-hour trip home. I say all of this with the deepest love and admiration for that woman. Allow The Children would not exist without my wife Sue.

We had been home for about a week, and we needed to buy Christmas gifts for our family. We went into our local Sam's Club in search of some bargains. As I pushed my cart down an aisle filled with Christmas merchandise, I spotted a pastor of a local church in our area. He was more than just a pastor; he was a longtime friend, and had been the missionary in Hungary that Sue and I had visited on the first mission trip we ever took out of the U.S. We would count him as a role model for us as we considered God's call on our own lives. When we got past the obligatory greetings, we began to talk about our new ministry. He asked us, "When are you going to come to our church and share your ministry with our people?" We had not ever shared this work outside of our own church, and we had a calendar that was wide open. The pastor assigned us a date in early January, and we were excited about this. As the date neared, the excitement turned to anxiety. We did not have a presentation. I was used to teaching, but mission presentations need to cast a vision and inspire people. The Sunday came, and we gave the worst missionary presentation in the history of western civilization.

Unlike many missionaries who speak in churches, Sue and I were not seeking personal support. God had provided this for us before He ever sent us out. As a businessman, I had a dream of retiring in my fifties and moving to a house on a lake where I could fish and enjoy myself for the balance of my life. I was right on track to do this when I took my trip to Asia in 1996. The dream went up in smoke. I could not break away from what God was moving me toward doing. I also did not have the excuse to use that I lacked the funding to do the ministry. That which was to retire me on a lake, now carried me to the ends of the earth.

Despite our terrible presentation, we did manage to get our story out about the little group of thirteen orphans. My mother had sponsored one of them, but twelve more remained. We had hoped to pick up one or two more sponsors for them at that church. At the end of the evening, we got another clear message about who was in charge of our ministry. Not only did that church pick up support for some of our ministries, but we left that evening with a sponsor for each one of those orphan children to whom I had so foolishly committed. We could not take an ounce of credit for this. We could only look to the Heavens and praise the Creator.

As the year of 2004 was moving into autumn, our ministry was growing rapidly. Sue was in Nepal, when we hit another crisis point. It had always been in the back of my mind that in a pinch, we could stop taking new children, and Sue and I could, perhaps, handle support of the number we had. The realization came that we had gone beyond our capacity to self-fund. In the early months, I did about fifteen minutes a week of receipting and bookkeeping on the computer in my office. The income was growing, but at this point, the need had gone ahead of the income. The office work time increased. Tracking of sponsors and children they sponsored became a bigger job. In looking at the financials, it became apparent that we were moving into dangerous territory. I was starting to wonder what we should do. Neither Sue nor I are good fund raisers. While Sue was out of town, I had received an e-mail at our Allow The Children address. This was a rare occurrence, since most folks that knew about our ministry knew us personally and used our personal e-mail address. The letter stated that the writer had picked our website out of the huge search engine list of ministry organizations, and felt led of God to send me $37.43. In a few days, an envelope came and true to his word, he had enclosed the check for the exact amount. I wrote him a thank you note, and assured him that all of the money he had sent would go to help the children and ministry partners overseas. The next day, I got another e-mail from this gentleman asking if he could speak with me on the phone. The phone connection was made, and he asked me several questions about my background and what our ministry was currently doing. At the end of our conversation, he said in very matter of fact terms, "I am going to send you a check for $10,000.00." I usually have many words to share, but I was speechless. In a few days, the envelope arrived, and there was his check for $10,000.00. Coincidentally, or Providentially, this filled the deficit we had at the time. Since I do not believe in coincidences, I could only praise God. I had heard stories like this from missionary friends, but here it was happening to us. We have had similar experiences over the years. It still amazes me every time it happens. These experiences are clear reminders to us that God is still on the throne, and we are still dwelling in His place of blessing for us.

As we moved forward on the path that God had created for us, my mother and grandmother regularly prayed for me and asked about my trips. My mother was sponsoring an orphaned child, and writing letters back and forth with her child. Most sponsors write one letter a year to their child. Since my mother knew Sue and I were traveling many times each year, she would have a letter ready each time we departed. My mother very much understood what it meant to be homeless and without adequate food and clothing. The relationship between my mother and her child lasted until the day my mother died. My grandmother who was in her nineties had begun to lose her vision and could no longer read. She took her Bible and my grandfather's Bible and gave them to me, saying, "Maybe you could take these overseas and give them to someone who could read them." I did take some Bibles overseas, but not those Bibles. I have those Bibles today. They are quite precious to me, and bring tears to my eyes as I read little notations she had jotted in the margins. Though never educated beyond elementary school, my grandmother did read through her Bible many times. The cover was worn out, and I know that many tears were shed in prayer during her times alone with her Lord. Much of that prayer was for me, and I cannot imagine what my life would have been without the godly mother and grandmother I had. I know they are both still smiling and likely mentioning me before the Lord personally now.

The Seasons of Life

Allow The Children was now like a toddler that Sue and I had birthed only a few years ago. It was growing every day, and it became more and more demanding of our time. We added the country of Burundi to our ministry purview. This ministry came with a couple from our church whose lives were consumed by overseeing this ministry for the next ten years. Sue wanted to reach other people profiles, and ministries were established in Bangladesh and in Central America. For a short while, we even helped some Palestinian Christians who were ministering to orphans. Our number of partners in Nepal continued to grow. One of our earliest expansions of the ministry in Nepal came when we received a set of photographs from a man that we knew but had not worked with in the past. Sue and I looked at the pictures, then looked at each other and at the same time declared these to be the saddest looking pictures we had ever seen. The children were very poorly dressed and malnutrition was obvious in the gaunt little faces and skinny little arms and legs. Just as it has been said that it is never a convenient time to have another child, so with a child sponsorship program, it is never a good time to take on twelve new children. We could not refuse, however, so some prayer time was invested as well. We did not realize at the time that the man, who brought us these sad looking children, would become our lead partner, administrator, and the example of a godly evangelist for us in the future. God provided sponsors for these children very quickly. Sue put together a montage of before and after pictures six months later, and it was totally amazing the transformation that could be seen in the small bodies and faces. We could only look on and thank God that He allowed us to be a part of what He was doing among the children in Nepal.

My dad went through a time of change in his early eighties. He had been seventy-four when we sold the restaurant business in 1999, and we had invested in real estate. He was the consummate entrepreneur and did not want to remain in the role of a passive investor. He took back a number of his properties from the management company and began to manage them himself. My son Mike and I helped him. I did his bookkeeping, which was not too big of a job. I was already doing Allow The Children's bookkeeping, and had the software to handle his. A big change happened when my dad turned eighty. He started redoing his estate plan and putting his financial house in order. When he was eighty-two, he shared with my mother and me that he would not be around the following year. When we asked him why, he pointed out that his father, his six brothers, and his uncles and cousins had never lived beyond eighty-three years. This seemed to be the Cook family heritage, and he was certain in his own mind that he would not live beyond this time. His eighty-third birthday came and went, and he was still alive. His eighty-fourth birthday came and went, and he still remained. He did, however, start to show some mild memory issues, but for eighty-four, that is not a surprising development.

My grandmother was now moving up in her nineties and her arthritis made grasping things with her hands nearly impossible. She took a bad fall at her assisted living facility, and after a period of rehab, she was transferred to an intermediate care facility which was close to my mother's house, but about 35-40 minutes away from where I lived. My mother and I had a regular schedule of visiting my grandmother on Wednesday and Saturday mornings. The food at the nursing home was bland, to accommodate most of the senior citizens who could not have salt or seasoning in their diet. My grandmother's doctor told her to eat all of the salt and seasoning she wanted. She never once had any issues with high blood pressure or high sugar levels. When we went to visit her, I always stopped by a drive thru and got her a cup of coffee and a sausage biscuit. She loved these, and I loved watching her get so much enjoyment from them. My grandmother's room was upstairs and down two long hallways. It was a pretty good hike to get there. My mother had bad knees, and could not make that walk. We parked her car, which had a handicap sticker, very near the front door. Just inside the front door of the nursing home was a little visiting area with tables and chairs. I would get my mother comfortably seated in a chair, and then make the hike to my grandmother's room. I then took my grandmother in her wheelchair down the long halls to the elevator. We would descend to the first floor. There, the elevator opened right by the little sitting area where my mother waited. As I wheeled my grandmother out, her eyes would meet my mother's eyes, and both of their faces would break into the biggest, most wonderful smile that I could imagine. They really didn't need to say a word. They just connected with their eyes and with their smiles. I knew what they had been through together, and the bond that still held. These were very rewarding times for me. Conversations were never earth shattering.

Perhaps some readers might ask, "Why, then, do we even need to know these details?" It is these small details of our lives that we will one day recall and wish we could restore. In our quest for happiness, we miss the little things that really do bring happiness to us, and chase after big ideas, that often only disappoint. Sometimes my mother would take a new blouse or pair of pants for my grandmother. She frequently cut up fresh fruit and took it to her. There was a piano in this little sitting area, and I would occasionally sit down and play a few of my grandmother's favorite hymns. The gifts that we all were giving to each other were time and memories. Our time together, our connection of love and our smiles of affirmation meant so much to us. I would continue these visits every week that I was not out of the country, until the day that my grandmother passed away. My mother would only make it part of the way.

I was leaving on Tuesday for a trip to Nepal and Bangladesh. I heard from my father on the Sunday before I left, that he had taken my mother to the hospital because of breathing trouble. The hospital had drawn a lot of fluid off of her lungs and scheduled her for tests the following week to determine the cause of this malady. When I returned from the trip three weeks later, I went to visit my mother at her home. She shared with me the bad news: She had cancer. Mom had been a breast cancer survivor fourteen years earlier. Despite the declaration at the time that she was cancer free after her treatments, a small bit of the cancer had managed to stay in her, and to slowly grow over the years.

My father really didn't like to go to doctors' offices. He always grumbled about wasting his valuable time sitting in the waiting room. My mother wanted someone to go with her to the many appointments she would now need to attend with the oncologist. I could help her fill out the paper work, do the computer check in, and most importantly, be with her when the doctor gave an analysis of her condition on that day. Many decisions were required along the way about starting and stopping different treatments and coordinating other medical care needed by my mother. When these decision points came up, my mother would turn to me and ask, "What do you think?" I would restate the doctor's options and her projected outcomes and perhaps ask how my mother would feel about these. We would always agree on the decisions, and it was a big encouragement to my mother to have this affirmation from someone that she knew was on her side. One of the traits that my mother had which I cherished so much over my lifetime was that she had always been on my side. I *could not* have missed this part of her journey for any reason. Being there for her was very important for me. It didn't occur to me at the time, but I was doing what I had learned to do *from* my mother. She was reaping the good fruit of what she had sown in my life over many years.

One morning, my mother called me and told me she would not be able to go with me to the nursing home to visit my grandmother. She had received a call from the nursing home and had been told that because of the flu outbreak, they were not recommending that people visit until the outbreak had passed. My mother, who was taking chemo therapy, had a highly compromised immune system, and would be very much at risk of not only contracting flu, but dying of flu if she got it. It was important to my mother that someone go to see her mother. I absolutely *had* to go. I couldn't stay away. When I arrived to visit my grandmother, the nursing home had a sign on the front door advising everyone that the facility was having a flu epidemic. When I went in the door and stopped at the desk to sign in, I was told that the section where my grandmother was living had nearly everyone sick with the flu. I was advised of the risk of going up there. I acknowledged the risk, but I knew that my grandmother looked forward to our twice weekly visits, so I decided to go on up and visit her. I was handed a surgical mask and advised to wear it all the while I was up there. I went on to the elevator and up to the second floor to my grandmother's room. I am not a big fan of surgical masks, so I removed it and went on in to her room. My grandmother's roommate was very ill and in her bed. My grandmother was sitting in her wheel chair like she always was, and was very happy to see me. We had talked for a little while when a nurse came in, wearing a full isolation room garb, complete with mask and hood. When she saw me sitting there, she was quite alarmed. She began to tell me about the flu outbreak. The Lord has blessed me with a pretty good resistance to disease, and I was willing to get the flu, if I must, to minister to my grandmother. When I travel to the countries in which I minister, I am regularly exposed to a number of dreaded diseases, including leprosy, tuberculosis, and yes, flu. History has shown us that the gospel penetrated the Roman Empire very rapidly, when the people saw Christians risking their lives to help those who had plague. A well-established principle in Scripture is, "God blesses us so that we can glorify Him by blessing others." Good health given to one by the Almighty is not for mere enjoyment. It is to be used to serve in whatever capacity the Lord has assigned us. Lest I sound too boastful, I must note that my grandmother, too, was sitting in a room with a flu patient, and she had on no mask or protective clothing. To live as long as she had lived, she had already been through many years of flu outbreaks, and survived. The quarantine lasted through my next visit, and neither my grandmother nor I contracted the flu. Thanks be to the Almighty!

From the very first visit with the oncologist, we were told that my mother's cancer would not be cured. The objective of her treatment would be to extend her life a little, and to make her life a little more comfortable. This would launch a journey of two-and-a-half years that I would take with my mother. I now count that time as the greatest two-and-a-half years I ever spent with her. The treatment began with a type of hormonal pill that would block the growth messages from the cancer. These were easily tolerated by my mother, and were effective for about a year or so. The first of these medications stopped working after several months, and a second one was tried. It, likewise, worked well for several months, before becoming ineffective. We were out of this type of medication, and would now need to begin chemo therapy. The options were somewhat limited here, because my mother was a diabetic, and had kidneys that would not tolerate many kinds of chemotherapy. A course of pills was begun. Each week we would return to the Cancer Center to have her blood tested and to find out what adjustments needed to be made. The amount of medicine was gradually being increased and we were starting to see a little decline in the cancer markers in her blood tests.

I left the country for a two week trip to Nepal. I didn't want to schedule a longer trip, because I wanted to be with my mother should anything change. I had been in Nepal only a day, when I received an e-mail from Sue. It said that my mother had a bad reaction to her medicine and was in the hospital. She was in very bad condition, and the doctors were saying that the family might want to gather around her. I fully trusted Sue to manage any details that needed to be handled with respect to my mother, and she said in her e-mail that if I wanted to stay and finish my ministry time in Nepal, that she would keep me informed and deal with whatever happened there. I did want to stay and finish what I was doing, but I could not. I needed to come home. Problem: This was Nepal. Flights in and out of Nepal were very limited, and I could not just drive to the airport and get on the next plane out. We got a flight scheduled for three days later, and I began the thirty hour trip home. I had booked my ticket through Delhi, India coming over, so I needed to go through there on the way home. Anyone who has had the pleasure of traveling through India knows that travelers need to be careful when someone offers to help them out of the goodness of his heart. The list of con games is endless, and they come from people on the streets and from workers in the airport. I was confronted by just such a situation when I arrived in Delhi to change planes after a six-hour layover. I was told by the man at the ticket counter that my flight had been canceled and that I could not reschedule for another forty-eight hours. He knew a good hotel where I could stay. What I am supposed to do here is to be grateful for his help and go with the transportation he arranges to the hotel. The cost of said transportation and hotel will be huge, and when I check in to my flight forty-eight hours later, I will find I am not booked on it, but my helper can get me out on another airline at a considerable cost. A call to Sue who checked with our travel agent revealed no problem with my flight. I was very unhappy with this agent, and told him loudly enough so that all surrounding people could hear, that people could go to jail in our country for dishonest acts like he had done. His whole attitude toward me changed. I was no longer an easy mark but someone who could cause him to lose face in a big time manner. After a wait, an agent from the airline on which I was booked came and called me to the desk. She then accompanied me through check-in and into my boarding gate. I made my flight home.

When I arrived home, I was told that my mother had made a miraculous turnaround. I knew that the prayers of people literally around the world had been answered while I was in flight. When I visited my mother in her hospital room, she was awake and happy to see me. She was somewhat apologetic for my trip being interrupted, but still happy to have me there. In a few days, my mother was ready to leave the hospital, but she needed several weeks of rehabilitation to build back her strength and balance which had been compromised by the bad reaction to the chemotherapy. In discussing with the medical personnel which rehabilitation center would be best, we learned that the nursing home where my grandmother was staying had one of the preferred facilities for rehabilitation. We transported my mother there. Once she was settled into her room, I went up the hall and up the elevator to my grandmother's room. She was a little surprised to see me on a day that was not my normal visiting day. I wheeled her down to my mother's room, and the two were quite delighted to see one another. Big smiles and hugs were exchanged. Both ladies had health adversity in their lives, but they had each other, and that was cause for great joy and satisfaction. I would make the trip daily to unite these two into one room. The blessing of their being essentially living together was a sweet irony. It is amazing how the Lord can take the worst possible circumstances and bring a wonderful surprise right in their midst.

After several weeks, my mother was discharged from rehab, and we resumed our twice weekly visits. My mother did not drive after this physical battle and she became a bit more dependent on my father and me. It was about this time that my mother started saying about my father, "He can't remember anything." She was starting to be concerned about him. This concern would grow as my mother's last days drew near. Nobody understood my father like my mother did. She knew exactly what was coming, and she was starting to make me aware of my father's memory problems.

My mother and I went to the oncologist for the first visit after her release from rehab. The burning question that needed to be answered was, "What do we do now for treatment, since we had the life-threatening reaction to the previous medication?" I suggested that we look at where the cancer markers were on the last blood test. As the oncologist looked at these, she was somewhat taken aback. The markers had dropped almost to zero. The medicine was working very well. Not knowing how we would react, she very gently stated that one option would be to restart the medicine at a much lower dosage. If we saw any sign of problem we would discontinue it. My mother, as she always did, looked to me for my thoughts. I weighed the pros and cons for her and we decided together to try this strategy. It turned out to be a good strategy, and it bought her another six or seven months of life. The medicine, however, like the previous treatments, would eventually lose its effectiveness.

The ministry at Allow The Children continued to grow and prosper. God brought some more very generous donors into our lives, which enabled us to double the number of children we were helping. The administrative and field work was increasing proportionally, and we had added some new staff missionaries who greatly helped in shouldering the load. Sue was spending nearly half of each year overseas, traveling in and out of each of our countries. I was continuing to take two week or shorter trips, and investing more time doing administrative work stateside. When I went into a country, I usually went right to work teaching and training pastors. I finished, and left to get back home as quickly as I could. If I ever had any sense that God couldn't get the work of the ministry done without me, it was certainly eradicated during this time. I had a sense that I needed to be around stateside. Looking back, it was necessary not only for my mother's needs, but for my dad's as well. He continued to go into his office and manage his rental units. I continued doing his bookkeeping and keeping things straight there. I also was able to pick up the slack for Sue at home while she traveled. It was necessary for her to spend greater amounts of time in countries where we were adding new children to our program.

Over a stretch of about six months, things seemed to be going well for my mother. The chemo that had so hurt her before was doing a wonderful job of keeping her cancer at bay. The day came, however, when it was no longer effective, and the cancer markers in my mother's blood started climbing again. We tried a couple of other chemo drugs, which didn't work. The doctor had tears in her eyes and she hugged my mother as we were leaving after what would prove to be our final visit to her office. She promised to call me with the latest test results, but she was not optimistic. On a Friday afternoon, while I was at my parents' house, the call from the oncologist came. She shared that we had no more medicines which my mother could take. I asked, "How long do you think my mother has?" Her reply was, "A few months at most."

My mother and I had been spending a lot of time together over the last two and a half years. Very often, my mother would give me instructions for her funeral. "I don't want to be laying up in front of the church with everyone looking at me. I don't want to be in my casket at the funeral home with everyone coming by saying how good my body looks." She was both adamant in her instruction to me, and fervent in her request that this be observed. It never occurred to me at the time that she was protecting both my father and her adopted daughter Whitney. Actually, it would make her funeral much easier on all of the family. It also did not occur to me that my mother was giving her funeral wishes to me, rather than to my father. All of us thought based upon my father's surface response that he was handling my mother's illness and pending death quite well. My mother knew, and we would learn later, he was not. My mother also gave a firm exhortation to me a number of times during this two-and-a-half year period. "When you see my body lying there, remember that it is not me anymore. It is just my dead body. I will be with Jesus in Heaven!" To those who would think an eighty-one-year-old mother educating her sixty-year-old missionary son about simple Bible truths was a bit superfluous, I would firmly protest. My mother was always a caregiver. She said, "I love you" in so many ways to her family. Well aware that her death would bring great sorrow to me, she wanted to redirect my thinking to the joyful truth of eternity for a child of God. I treasure these exhortations in my heart to this day.

As I shared the oncologist's prognosis with my parents, my mother affirmed her faith and her submission to the Lord's will for her life. My father was mostly silent. He did not make gestures of comfort or say anything encouraging. That was never his style that I could remember, but this seemed like a good time to deviate from that style. I really had no idea what was going on. I am a lot like my father, in that I am usually private with my emotions. That which most people would interpret as great emotional strength is actually great emotional fragility. The responses I made were much more along the lines of cutting through the anxiety in the room, and doing what was the needed and right thing. As I sat there thinking, the context of my thoughts were in a two month time frame. I left and drove home, thinking in the same manner.

The next day, I picked up my mother and we went to visit my grandmother. At my mother's request, we did not share the oncologist's news with my grandmother. I did not know at the time, that the smiles that lit up these two ladies' faces would be their last together. Indeed, no one but my mother could bring that smile to my grandmother's face. This was the last time they ever saw each other on this side of Heaven. On the way home, my mother asked me to stop at the dollar store so she could fill up on laundry detergent. She used a certain brand from there, which came in a big bottle, too heavy for her to get off of the shelf. We bought a goodly supply. I later discovered that my mother had frozen a lot of fruit and apple sauce, which was a favorite of my father, and of all of our family. She had also made a new quilt for each family member, and left these quilts in a trunk with each labeled with the respective family member's name.

My mother was ever the caregiver, and she worked overtime to be able to care for her family even *after* she had departed. She was buying laundry detergent as a way of having everything in good shape for when she would no longer be there. Per her usual habit, my mother fixed my favorite grilled cheese and tomato soup for lunch that Saturday. This would be the last of those special times that we would share together.

The following week was a very busy one for me. In addition to my sixtieth birthday which would be on Wednesday, I had our semi-annual Board of Directors meeting on Friday. Preparation for this board meeting took some time. I talked with my mother by phone early in the week. Very early Wednesday morning, I got a call from my father informing me that my mother was having pain and trouble breathing. My father, who was always at his office by 4:00 a.m. had come home when she called him, and he was not certain what to do. I told him to hang up and dial 911. I would meet them at the hospital. When I got to the hospital, the ambulance had just unloaded my mother, and my father was giving the information to the triage nurse. We were taken back to a bay, where my mother was hooked up to some monitors which measured various vital signs. After a few minutes, my father asked me, "Are you going to be here for a while?" When I replied in the affirmative, he said, "I think I will go on back over to the office. You can call me if anything comes up. At eighty-six years of age, my father was still as driven by his work as he had been at forty-six years of age. I didn't really consider at the time that this set of circumstances with my mother was more than he could process. Getting out of the hospital and leaving me there to look after my mother was his best method of coping with this very painful and confusing set of circumstances. I sat the usual two to three hours in the emergency room bay with my mother. She was taken down to X-ray, and had some fluid drained off her lungs. She was also given some pain medication which made her sleep off and on most of the time. Finally, the hospital doctor admitted her, and we were taken up to a room on the medical floor. Our ER has no cell phone service, so when I arrived upstairs, e-mails and texts started ringing in. A text from my wife simply said, "Happy birthday, wherever you are!" I have a wonderful wife. I called her and filled her in on what was going on, and she said that a birthday

Michael Cook

celebration didn't have to be exactly on one's birthday. She also gave me an un-needed exhortation that I should give this time to my mother.

The day was one of sitting by my mom's bed, with her sleeping most of the time. I sat in deep thought and prayer, often not even aware of the surroundings myself. She would wake up, groggy from the pain medication and would look around for something familiar. She would call my name, "Mike!" I instinctively would say, "Yes Mam!" and would be right there taking hold of her hand in a flash. She had taught me when I was a small child, to respond to her immediately when she called my name. This was no longer an act of obedience, but an act of love. I don't remember when the transition took place, but I thank the Lord that I had a mother who taught me to respond when she called. If one does not learn this response in life, he will never be able to function in a job with a boss, or respond to a life's call from the Almighty.

It is no coincidence that in the Ten Commandments, the fifth commandment says to honor one's father and mother. The first four commandments deal with our responding toward God and the last five deal with our interactions with those around us. The last five won't happen to their fullest, unless the first five are in order.

Late in the day, the doctors came in and told me that they had no real treatment for her. They said that her death could come at any time. I had a choice of either letting her stay in the hospital for a few days, or taking her home. They recommended that I talk with the hospice people who would do everything needed to assure that my mother had the maximum amount of comfort in her final days. Because of the late hour, it was decided that my mother would be discharged the next day. We would arrange to have a hospital style bed brought to her house, and have her transported by ambulance back to her house, since she was weak, and on pain meds which made her mobility very shaky. This was all accomplished the next morning, and we had my mother home, in a hospital bed that had been set up in her family room. Several of us gathered around her. The hospice nurse came by late in the day and my mother was given much stronger pain medicine. The cancer had raced into her lungs, her liver, and some bones. She had born up under a great deal of pain. That evening, I hugged my mother good-bye and told her I loved her for the last time as I headed home. My son Mike and his wife Heather arranged to stay with my mother on Friday as I was tied up all day with our board meeting. Heather is a nurse practitioner, and was able to give medication to my mother during the day. We were about an hour from the end of the meeting, and I was talking to the board about our increased emphasis on training of national workers in our countries where we ministered. Sue stepped out into the hall to take a phone call. She came in and interrupted me mid-sentence and said she needed to speak to me outside. I knew immediately what this meant. I turned the meeting over to one of the board members, and headed over to my mother's house. My mother had just passed from this life. I had prayed over the last few days that God would not allow her to suffer long. He had taken her home in a few short days. My loss was Heaven's gain.

When I arrived at my parent's home, my mother's body lay peacefully in the hospital bed. I went over and kissed her on the forehead, and she was still warm. I sat in the family room with Dad, Whitney, Mike, Heather, and Sue. The funeral home arrived after about an hour. The man who had come to transport my mother's body suggested that everyone should avail themselves of the opportunity to go into another room while he loaded the body. There is no easy and gentle way to load a body, and the shock of seeing ones loved one put into a body bag and hauled out is unnerving for many people. Everyone went into the kitchen area; everyone except me. I told the funeral home worker that I wanted to stay. As he first began to bring the bag around the body, I thought everything inside of me was going to explode. Waves of panic, sadness, and depression all welled up inside of me. Then, Mom's exhortation came racing into my mind as she knew that it would: "When my body is lying there, it is not me. I am in heaven with Jesus!" I cannot start to adequately describe the wave of peace, control and joy that flooded in and totally erased all of the negative feelings. I was thankful that I had that assurance that she was now better off than I was. She no longer suffered from the excruciating pain. She could breathe in a breath of heavenly air without any struggle at all.

A Hospice nurse who had stayed in contact with me asked if I wanted her to break the news to my grandmother. I absolutely did not. I felt strongly that I should be the one to talk with her. My mother and I had missed our Wednesday visit, so Nanny knew something was amiss. When I shared with her that my mom had passed away, she was not surprised. She really didn't have much of an emotional reaction. She began to reassure me that my mother was better off in Heaven. Like my mother, Nanny always sought to care for the other person, even more than her own self. She was much more concerned with how I was doing. I would continue my twice weekly visits with her until the day she died. I was basically her only relative left alive that kept in constant touch with her.

Mike and I took my dad to the funeral home the next day to sign papers and finalize the details for the funeral. My parents had prepaid most everything, so there was not a lot of paperwork to do. This was a tremendous blessing, since my father was really not up to this. We talked with Pastor Clarkson and laid out the funeral details. Pastor Clarkson was my parents' pastor and my dad's best friend. Per my mom's wishes, we scheduled only a brief family time for those who wanted to see my mother one more time. This lasted about forty-five minutes. Looking back now, what I thought was controlled emotional strength on my dad's part was a continued inability to process all of the thoughts and feelings that were running through his mind. He had just lost his life partner of sixty-two years. He now had to take on the responsibility of getting an eighteen-year-old through her senior year of high school, and on to college. He was without the person who kept everything at home running smoothly. He was lonely, afraid, and depressed. That is a very normal reaction, but the ability to think through all of these and carefully sort out what he could change from what he could not was beyond him. When dealing with our elder loved ones, we must never presume that what we see on their faces is what is going on inside of them. For the fittest of us, emotional pain can drain us completely. In our youth, we have the strength and energy to fight back, and we do so. For many in their late eighties or early nineties, they do not.

Our next gathering was at graveside. The family came together with Pastor Clarkson to commit my mother's body to the earth, and to rejoice that she was in Heaven. We left a great deal of our sadness at the grave.

The next day, we had a celebration of life service for my mother. I spoke about her love for her Lord, her love for her family, and how she had been our caregiver up to the very end. Heather sang a beautiful song entitled *Celebrate Me Home* which totally captured what we were doing. Pastor Clarkson preached a message and invited all to receive Christ like my mother had done many years before. At the end of the service, we received visitors at the front of the church. I had a chair set up for my father, who could not have stood for an hour under these circumstances. With my mother's body already interred, rather than sitting in an open casket behind us, the interaction with people who came was much easier. Following this time of visitation, the good people of Temple Baptist Church served our family a wonderful meal. The funeral guidelines that my mom had laid out protected us all from a lot of the stress that so many families go through when they bury a loved one. She was our caregiver to her very last day, and even beyond.

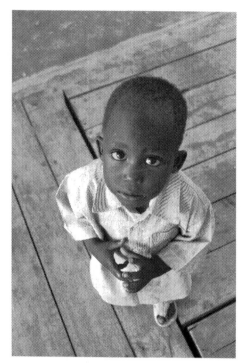

Can't say no

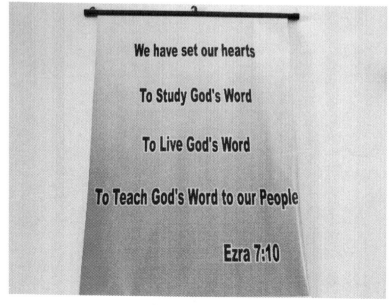

Focus of our training of leaders

Mother and father on their 50th wedding anniversary

Grandmother and grandfather on their 50th wedding anniversary

Mike and Sue Cook

The privilege to attend school

Reaching out to help the blind children

What do I do now?

Allow The Children was adding new ministries, and from time to time, closing out some ministries that no longer were fruitful or a good fit for us. Ministries, just like our lives, go through change continually. God continued to financially bless the organization, and we were able to minister in ever larger ways. I began to have a bit of a problem with my other "ministry." I say ministry, because one learns that when his parents age, they will have needs that someone must meet. If I was willing to go around the world to minister to folks, I certainly should be willing to go across town to minister to my family. My father, who was struggling with his loss of my mom, became more detached each month that passed. He wanted to be at his office as much as possible. To that end, he broke business relationships with our property management company, and announced that he would now manage all of our combined rental properties. This would require a lot of extra time and work for me. Additionally, it was substantially less profitable; since we were not equipped properly to make this change.

A difficult struggle within my spirit would continue for the next four years. I had no doubt that I was called to work alongside the believers in the countries where God had taken me. At the same time, my dad needed me. He would not acknowledge that he needed anyone, but his life was becoming more chaotic. He became suspicious of the legal and financial professionals he had worked with for many years. He and my mother had a very complex estate plan that he could no longer understand. His issues would continue to grow over the next few years. Even though he controlled a great deal of wealth, my dad began to believe that he was out of money. His depression era upbringing put him into survival mode. He would forget where he had placed something, and would immediately accuse someone of stealing it. This became stressful for family and workers who were in contact with him.

My father, like my mother, had grown up in Madison County, North Carolina during the depression and war years. One of seven sons born to a farmer and his wife, my father lived in abject poverty like most everyone else in the county. Medical care was available, but limited. My father had diphtheria as a child. The doctor, who serviced a large area, left my father's side one evening, saying that if the fever did not break, my dad would be dead by morning. Providentially, the fever broke, and he survived. Madison County was a dead end of poverty and hardship. My dad knew by the time that he entered his teens that he wanted to get out of that place. From the day he did leave until the day he died, he had no desire to return there to live. Further, he instructed us not to take his remains there to be buried in the family cemetery. He somehow had a God-given instinct to rise out of the poverty and become something different.

My dad had a very early knack for numbers that would serve him well in the business world years later. As the family harvested their tobacco crop each year, my grandfather assigned him the extra job of counting what they had hung in the barn. According to my grandfather, he was "always right on the money." At age thirteen, Dad received Christ in a revival meeting at a local church. Madison County was known for violence, for poverty, and for alcohol. As a dry county, no alcohol could be sold legally. Liquor was manufactured in homemade stills, and every farmer had his own supply of Mason jars for holding the product. The sheriff of the county could be bought for a price. If a person did not pay, he would break up his still, and seize the liquor. Interestingly, the sheriff's office kept the confiscated liquor, and dispensed it to people for "medicinal purposes." All one had to do was bring an empty Mason jar with a few herbs in the bottom down to the Sherriff's office and he would fill it up. I had numerous ancestors who treated their chronic illness daily with medicine from the Mason jar. My dad came to clearly understand that the violence and poverty were made all the worse by the drinking problem. He pledged early to himself that he would not be a drinker, and he never was. My mom's step-father was reluctant at first to allow his daughter to go out with the likes of my dad. The Cook boys were known for being violent, for drinking and for driving their cars too fast. My dad successfully demonstrated that he was different, and was permitted to court her.

There is absolutely no question that my father's environment and circumstances while he was growing up shaped who he became as a man. When the time came for him to take his wife and children out of the mountains into the city, he jumped at the opportunity. He went from doing whatever farm work he could find to working three jobs in the city of Cleveland, Ohio. The reason he worked only three jobs was that he needed to get four or five hours of sleep each night. After several years of these hours, he hired on with a retail grocery chain, and began a climb up the corporate ladder, which culminated in his being in charge of the Auditing Department. The young boy who could so deftly track stalks of tobacco hung in the barn, had grown into a man who could track the inventory of over five-hundred stores, right to the last penny's worth. He was very successful, but he also developed into a classic "workaholic." This would stay with him until the day he died. When he was sick in a hospital bed, only weeks from his death, he kept asking us to help him get up out of the bed so he could go to work. The depression year's struggle for survival in Appalachia when he was young, very strongly imprinted itself on his psyche, and it could never be erased.

In his first few years of life in Cleveland, Dad became enamored with the stock market. He used to go to the brokerage at lunch time just to watch the ticker tape. He had the ability to numerically evaluate a company, and he began to invest. In his lifetime, Dad made as much from the stock market as he made from all of his jobs combined. He had the ability to make good decisions in the market, and the confidence in his ability to invest his hard earned money.

Very soon after we moved to Cleveland, we began to attend a church called Euclid Nottingham Baptist Church which was on the lakeshore just outside of Cleveland. My parents came under the discipleship of Dr.

Alan Lewis, the pastor. Dr. Lewis had grown up on the mission field in Africa. He would later leave this church to become the president of Baptist Mid Missions, a large mission board with workers worldwide. My parents already had a bent toward missionaries, and they got to be a part of a church that was very active in supporting missionaries. From my early memories, I recall hosting furloughed missionaries in our home when they came to speak at our church. The stories they told were exciting, but quite honestly, I never, ever had a desire to travel to distant lands, and I especially did not want to go to a place that had jungles. All the same, my parent's experience with missionaries when they were growing up certainly transferred into who they were as adults. It also had an impact on me that I would only appreciate much later in my life.

I remember my father becoming a leader in the boys group at our church. He would ultimately head up the entire program. He was also my pride in the father/son softball games. All fathers were required to bat left handed if they were a natural right hander, and vice versa. My father had played a lot of baseball from the time he grew up. Because his family did not own the land that would have been left field for their baseball diamond, he and all of his brothers had to learn to bat left handed. My father became a true switch hitter, able to bat left handed or right handed equally well. When he came to bat in the father/son games, he always hit a home run. He would first hit a home run left handed. The other team would insist that he bat right handed next time. He would then hit a home run right handed. My favorite Major League baseball player of all time was Mickey Mantle, who was a switch hitter. I had a wonderful role model in my dad, and my natural instincts were to emulate him in many things. I can only thank the Lord for allowing me to grow up under my dad's mentorship.

When my father got his promotion in the company, we moved to a different town that was nearer to the Akron area than to the Cleveland area. We joined a small church that had just been started. My father very soon became quite active. He was chairman of the deacon board, as well as a teacher for many adult groups. When we left Ohio, to open the family's first fast food restaurant in Lynchburg, Virginia, my mother and father quickly joined a church, and once again, my father became an active and well-loved member. I have my father's Bible now, and it is totally worn out from the reading and study he put in. There are pages of notes with it as well, which show how he approached his studies to teach. It is both scary and joyful to see the way my father's study of God's Word has shaped my own life. I developed a similar pattern of study in my own life.

Just like my mother who had been touched by a missionary to Madison County, so my father also had a missionary come into his life. This missionary came and lived among the people. He farmed like everyone else. He taught these backwoods people how to terrace their hillside farms to prevent soil erosion and to increase their productive acreage. He also became a teacher at the local school, and taught Bible to the people when he had the opportunity. He became my dad's role model. His life was very different, and my dad could see that it was more productive and more joyful than the lives of the rest of the men in the community. The impact of this missionary to Madison County helped to shape what my father's life would look like for many years to come. My father always encouraged me to go into business, which I did. His unspoken encouragement, however, was toward spiritual things which he had pursued. I used my God given gifts to build up my church as best I could, and I especially enjoyed helping the missionaries of our church. A work that was started by a missionary to Appalachia two generations before I was born had sown seeds that were now firmly rooted in my heart.

I developed routines which enabled me to help my aging dad with what he needed while still devoting some time to Allow The Children. I took trips, but these were short and to the point. My son Mike and my dad's office manager kept things on track while I was out of country.

Allow The Children developed a new logo. This was the second logo change we had made in our history. I liked the first one, but the younger people said it made us look like a mom and pop outfit, so I was shouted down. The interim logo had a more upscale look, but I never got used to it. I did like, and still do like the new logo, because it has been associated with our updated mission statement, "Loving His Children, Building His Church." This perfectly describes who we are. We are used by God as

He pours out His love on His children. We are also used by Christ as He builds His church. Our brothers and sisters in our ministry countries cry out not only for help for their children, but for help and teaching in their churches. Each time I traveled to a new country, I spent time with the lead pastor in that area, in an effort to discern the needs of the believers there. Without fail, every one of them told me that the greatest need was for someone to come and teach them God's Word. Our early mission's career had emphasized this, and God was now bringing us more teaching opportunities than we had ever imagined. I began a regular teaching program in Nepal. The first few times I taught, I brought a short prepared lesson, but spent most of my time asking the church leaders what they would like to be taught. I was shocked that one of the leading requests was for teaching on giving. Almost anyone reading this right now would have more resources than every church leader in that room combined. Poverty is epidemic in the areas where I go. These men, however, wanted to study what God said about giving. Most North American Christ followers don't really have to take a big step of faith when they give. They trust their job or their bank account for their next meal. In a very poor country, survival is often a day by day affair. What you have in your hand in the morning, you will likely spend to feed your family that day. Giving to the church, to missions, or to some other work of the Lord is a very big step of faith.

Each of our current training programs was started in a unique way, in partnership with a lead pastor who has ministered to the others regularly. All have grown into programs where the needs are being met for basic Bible knowledge Answers to the questions with which they have struggled are being given. Invariably, the question and answer portion of my teaching is the highlight. I love getting questions from those who have been seeking understanding of perplexing issues. One type of question I have regularly been asked concerns false doctrines that have been taught by visiting speakers or by clerics of the prevailing local religion. From the very first day I took questions from those I was teaching, I would regularly make the statement, "It doesn't matter what I think. It only matters what the Word of God says." In an amazing way that I don't totally understand, the Lord has enabled me to recall Scriptures and respond to the questions I am asked. There is no doubt that the many hours invested by my parents in helping me to memorize and to understand scripture have produced some fruit. Rearing me in the church and introducing me to many godly pastors and missionaries also helped to establish a firm biblical grasp. In my adult years, I sat under good teachers, and I spent time alone in the Word each day. This has given me what the church leaders in so many countries have not had the opportunity to gain. Regardless of what God gives His servant or what blessing He bestows, it is not for personal consumption alone. Blessings are given to bless others and to glorify God in the process. Without this understanding, Allow The Children would not exist today.

I went to the nursing home one Saturday morning for my usual visit with Nanny. She did not recognize me when I came in. She had a blank stare on her face, and kept moving her hands as if she were shelling beans. I spoke to her, and she responded to me as if I were her younger brother, Troy. She continued this pattern through my entire visit. I went to the nurse's station, and talked to the nurse, who told me that Nanny had a urinary tract infection. She went on to say that it was very common in elderly people to go into a state of dementia when suffering from this type of infection. I checked back later, and learned that although they were treating her infection, they felt it best to admit her to the hospital. Nanny was taken to the hospital and placed in a room. She was quite a bit weaker, and scarcely knew anyone. A friend of hers came by the hospital every day and fed her. She was a great help to my grandmother. A group of hospice workers, including a doctor, a nurse, and a social worker met with me. Nanny had been on the hospice care list for over a year, due to a congestive heart failure condition. They had believed a year previously that she would not live more than a few months, and she already had proven them wrong. They said that my grandmother, this time, would certainly die and that the best thing to do was to stop all treatment of her infection and let her go.

I asked the doctor about the comfort factor. When Nanny had a urinary tract infection, she was very uncomfortable. Hospice was supposed to make people who were dying feel as comfortable as possible. The nurse, who had been quiet to this point, spoke up and agreed with what I was saying. They continued to treat the infection, and it got better. Ultimately, because they continued this treatment, she recovered from the infection, regained her strength and mental faculties, and was discharged from the hospital to the nursing home. She would live another fifteen months, and be a tremendous blessing to me. It is very scary to think that an option of stopping treatment in her case was even offered to me. This was not a case of taking heroic measures with artificial life support equipment to halt the course of nature for a few more months. This was depriving a very old person of her life, for no other reason than it seemed like an opportune time. Three years later, I would face a similar choice with my father, but with much different factors, decisions, and outcomes.

Allow The Children continued to add countries. In January of 2013, we traveled for the first time to the country of Haiti. I visited Nanny before I left on the trip. I kissed her on the forehead as I left her room, and told her I would see her in a week. She would pray for me while I traveled, as she always did. Haiti was Haiti. It was a mess from a major earthquake. It was a mess from a Category 4 hurricane. It was a mess from a cholera outbreak. It was a mess from years of political corruption. People in the capital city still lived in tents, and buildings reduced to rubble still lay untouched in the streets.

The spiritual condition of the country also lay in rubble. Despite countless individuals and agencies that have ministered there, the church is *not* strong. The same level of dependency and helplessness that plagues the culture also plagues the church. We met a lead pastor who would be our primary contact, and checked into a guest house in Port au Prince. Our week's agenda included visiting some orphanages, talking with a lady who wanted to take in abandoned little girls, and ministering to the lead pastor and his church. Of the contacts we made on the trip, only the lead pastor and the lady starting up the children's home panned out as long-term working partners for us. Two orphanages that we visited, on the surface did appear to have needy children living in needy conditions, but they turned out to be fraudulent business enterprises to enrich the men who were claiming to do such a good work. The huge number of ministries that have gone in and out of Haiti over the years has actually taught numerous people how to play the foreign aid game.

We have come to partner with several other very good ministries in Haiti over the past several years. The principle we have practiced over the years is to find someone who God is already using to do a work, and join efforts with that one to better equip and enable *that* ministry. We show up to participate in what God is doing, and seek to be used by God to bless and strengthen the ministries which are involved in the Lord's work.

It is quite amazing to think about how God takes total strangers from very different cultures and instantly bonds them together as if they had known one another all of their lives. Sue and I had immediate clarity about the pastor God had chosen as our primary partner in Haiti. That pastor announced to me on Saturday afternoon that I would be the guest speaker at his church's Sunday morning service. I am used to this after twenty-plus years of international ministry. The Lord opens my eyes to look around, opens my ears to hear, and opens my heart to receive His word. The pastor, in his conversations with me, talked about his desire to be a "Full Gospel" church. This term is fraught with a variety of implications. To a theologian, it likely describes a particular movement that exists in Christendom. To others, it usually means that the person wants to be and do everything necessary to fulfill salvation. I was pretty sure that this pastor meant the later. Countries like Haiti that are overcome by great spiritual and social problems often have a very confused theology underlying the problems. Indeed, so many different agencies and preachers from North America pass through Haiti that the entire spectrum of theology, from proper to flawed, has been set forth for the pastors to try to unscramble. Their heart's desire is to please the Lord, but they have had so much conflicting input, that they are confused. The root cause of this lack of understanding is a lack of training, and a lack of a solid mentors to disciple them. Having roots in Appalachia enabled me to see many men from the mountains called to preach at a very young age. Some, as young as fourteen or fifteen years old, would simply drop everything and began to travel a circuit; preaching at any little church or campground that would gather a crowd. They all lacked the training and ability to totally grasp all of the main theological concepts of the Bible. A variety of strange church practices have found their way out of these meetings, including such things as the "snake handling movement," which is still practiced in the county where I was born. Where theological confusion reigns, social and spiritual confusion reign, whether it is in Appalachia or in Haiti. I believed that for the morning message, God wanted me to speak from Ephesians 2. The first ten verses of this chapter lay out the concept of salvation by grace, through faith, which is the "full gospel" in practical terms. The chapter shows us all as helpless sinners, unable to save ourselves. Though we did not deserve any help, as we stood condemned to eternal death, God, purely out of His own graciousness, reached down and rescued us. We did not even have the faith necessary to receive this gift of grace, and God supplied us with that as well. No man has the right to boast of how he brought about or augmented his own salvation. It is entirely the Lord's work, and is freely extended to us as a gift. I spoke this as a teacher, as simply and plainly as I could. I am not a good "fire and brimstone" preacher. My style is much more suited as a teacher than as a firebrand preacher. Since I was preaching through a translator, I ended my message, and allowed the pastor to close with whatever challenge or application that he chose. He stepped forward and simply asked in the people's native Creole language, "Who needs to come to Jesus this morning?" I had studied French in college, and was able to understand what the pastor had asked. A woman toward the back of the room raised her hand, and the pastor instructed her to come to the front of the church. A man sitting closer to the front also raised his hand, and was invited to the front. They both knelt at the front of the church, and individually acknowledged Jesus Christ as the Lord of their lives. I had just been retaught something. It is not the preaching that brings someone to Christ. It is the Word of God applied to the heart by the Holy Spirit of God. As I had just taught, man is the recipient of a gift, not the participant by his own word or deed. I was thrilled that God had used me as a mouthpiece to speak His word. I fully understood that I had no other role in the salvation of these two souls.

Sue and I returned to the United States on Monday evening. We both agreed that there were ministry opportunities in Haiti, for a small agency like Allow The Children. The big agencies were doing a lot of big works, but so many small needs slipped through the cracks. Our focus of helping believers help others was quite different from the prevailing methodology of mass foreign aid. Our Haiti ministry now includes working with orphans through partners in Haiti, and training Haitian pastors who can, in turn, train others in the right theology that is so needed in Haiti.

Early Tuesday morning, I decided to go and visit Nanny. Ordinarily, I would go on Wednesday, but I hadn't seen her in over a week, and I really desired to be with her. I knew that she had prayed daily for me while I was in Haiti, and I wanted to share with her what we had done there. I was nearly there when my cell phone rang. My car enables me to answer on a hands free speaker. The caller was a hospice nurse who I had talked with a few times about my grandmother's health. What she said was like a kick in the gut to me. "Your grandmother is very near death." She went on to say that Nanny had asked if I had gotten back from my trip safely. I informed the nurse that I was, indeed, back from the trip, and was less than ten minutes away from the nursing home. I arrived at the nursing home and quickly made my way up the elevator and down the hall to my grandmother's room. The nurse greeted me with the sad words, "She is gone." She then continued, "Your grandmother wanted me to call and make sure you were home safely. When I assured her that you were, she closed her eyes and passed away." This still brings tears to my eyes as I am writing this many years later. My one-hundred- year-old grandmother, my greatest prayer warrior, the uneducated grandmother who had taught me to "just trust in the Good Lord," was gone. Before she would let herself rest, she needed to care for her grandson one last time. The two old ladies were now smiling at one another again, this time in heaven.

I left the nursing home very soon, after kissing Nanny's still warm forehead and squeezing her hand. As her remaining next of kin, I retreated into my comfortable administrator role, scurrying about making all of the arrangements for her funeral.

Nanny's funeral was patterned after Mom's funeral. We met as a family at the funeral home for viewing. The next day, we came as a family to the graveside for a short service conducted by Pastor Clarkson. He had visited Nanny regularly while she was in the nursing home, and Nanny had asked him to do her funeral service when she died. The next day, we had her celebration of life service at my church. Nanny had been a member of our church for many years, so a lot of people came to this service. In the weeks and months ahead, I would greatly miss our twice weekly times together. I would also come to miss her continued prayers for me.

In May of that year, Sue and I traveled to Israel with a group from our church. At the end of this great tour, we split off from the group and went to visit some ministries in the Palestinian territories. Palestinian Christians are under great pressure. They are persecuted by the Palestinian Muslims, and they feel the wrath of Israeli Defense Forces when the Muslim fighters lash out at the Israelis. Those Palestinian Christians who *could* migrate out of the area to Europe or North America have already left. Churches that were once very large now have only a few Christians remaining. Sue and I stayed in a very modern hotel in the West Bank. It was run by a Christian. We were the only guests. There simply are no people traveling in and out of West Bank, except crazy missionaries like us. We did some short term relief work, but our attempts to establish long term ministry there were thwarted by the lack of stability and a strong partner relationship. It is very chilling, however, to know that we have brothers and sisters in Christ who live under such pressure.

When we arrived home, Sue and I literally unpacked, washed our clothes, and repacked them for a trip less than a week later. We were now into June, and Allow normally does pastor training in June or July every year in Nicaragua. The trip was good. I was able to see a man come to Christ in an evening service that I preached. This man had spent time in America, but had never heard the Gospel during that time. Our time in Nicaragua is always very sweet, but this seemed to be one of the best times we had ever experienced.

During the trips to Israel and Nicaragua that Sue and I had taken, I seemed to have lost my appetite. I was having some urinary discomfort. I had my annual physical scheduled for the day after I returned from Nicaragua. Sue met a team in Guatemala, so I went home alone. At the physical, the usual blood work was done and vital signs taken. The doctor came into the examining room and sat down. Having been blessed all my life with good health, I expected to review the good test results, maybe encouraged to lose weight, and scheduled for a return next year. The doctor prefaced his remarks by saying, "I know this is supposed to be an annual physical, but we need to talk about something much more important today." He then said in a very sobering tone, "Your kidneys are shutting down. If we cannot discover what is causing this and correct it right away, you will be on dialysis or worse by next week." Okay, so now he definitely had my attention. I was sent immediately for a series of scans of my urinary tract. From there, I was sent to the Outpatient Department, to have a catheter inserted. I had sent off a text to Sue in Guatemala. She texted back just as the preparations for the procedure were happening. Sue is a Registered Nurse, and she better understood just how serious things were. This was Friday afternoon at quarter to five.

At daylight the next morning, Sue would take one group of short term travelers to the airport, and pick up a second group for the coming week. On the spot, she called and booked herself outbound for home, leaving one of our staff missionaries on the trip to coordinate the next team. At the time, I did not know that she had been able to do this. I left the hospital after the treatment, with instructions on how to manage the catheter, orders of what to do and not do, and appointments to see my primary care doctor on Monday and a urologist on Tuesday. I arrived home exhausted and emotionally drained from the day.

Prayer came easy that night, but sleep did not. I had questions, but no answers from the medical community. I did nothing but sit at home all day on Saturday. I was struggling with the catheter and struggling emotionally with this thing that was happening-totally out of my control. Trusting God and living in His peace is such a simple task, but it is one of the hardest things for us to do. Our physical bodies seem to be hard wired to fight against trouble or to flee from it if the odds don't seem favorable. That evening, I couldn't get to sleep in my bed, so I went into the living room and reclined on the sofa. Sleep still evaded me, and I was wide awake around midnight when I saw the headlights of a vehicle coming down my driveway. In just a minute, I received a text from Sue, saying, "Come open the back door." She had made it home. I did not know she was coming, but in the back of mind I certainly longed to have her at home with me. Having a partner like Sue with me, cut the burden I was carrying in half. With Sue there, I suddenly had a sense of confidence that "we" could beat this whole medical issue. What I had viewed as an unsurmountable obstacle now was reduced to a little speed bump. I lay down and slept quite well for the balance of the night. When the Lord chose Sue to be my spouse, He knew all of my weaknesses, and fully equipped Sue to offset those with her strengths. Only eternity will tell all of the ways she has impacted my life.

The appointment with my doctor on Monday had mixed news. The doctor had been testing my Creatinine level. A normal range should have been about 0.85 for me. It had been that way for years. The previous Friday when my doctor set things into motion, the level was at 4.7, which was very disturbing. On this Monday, it had dropped to 3.9, so it looked like the intervention thus far was helping. That was good. On the other hand, what had caused them to go up? The catheter was a temporary fix. What would be a permanent fix? I went to the urologist's office the next day wondering what answers he could give me. Did I have cancer? Would I be undergoing radical surgery or radical chemical treatments? The urologist rendered his findings to me. The problem could be surgically corrected. That was the good news. The bad news was that until my Creatinine level had fallen to at least 1.5, the surgery would be too risky to attempt. Ultimately, I would have to wear the catheter all summer long. In September, the surgery was done, and this fixed my problem. I was freed from the restricted lifestyle that I had lived for the past three months.

This health issue was a very humbling experience. My self-reliance was greatly diminished by this condition, and my reliance upon the Lord and the prayers of His people became so much more personal for me. Over the months I had people from all of our ministry areas praying fervently for me. I received e mails inquiring as to my progress. "How was I feeling? Was I improving? Would I soon come to teach?" Our pastor and some of my friends from our church came by the house to visit during the days when it was difficult for me to leave the house. My son Mike helped me set up a laptop at home, and transfer the company books from my dad's business office to my house. Even when I could not leave the house, I could keep the books straight. After my three months of treatment and a surgical procedure, I was able to travel again, and resume other day to day activities. I look back on this experience, and understand that God wanted to bring my focus more fully on Him.

Sue and I were able to make a short trip to Nepal the next summer. We so rarely get to travel together, so this was a very pleasant treat for me. On this trip, we talked with one of our long term partners about his newest ministry direction. He wanted to help "at risk" children in the slums of Kathmandu. He laid out his vision to us, and took us to the slum where we saw the early fruit of this vision. An AWANA Club that he had started in the slum area, had grown, and ultimately brought many adults as well as children under the sound of the Gospel. Out of this AWANA club, a church of two hundred people had been started. Sue would visit this area again in a few months, and a new children's home for street kids would be established. Little boys as young as seven years old, who had been abandoned to live on the streets, were taken into this children's home. There, for the first time, they had all of the food and clothing they needed. They were safe from the dangers of street life. They went to school regularly. They also heard the Gospel for the first time.

I also had the opportunity to travel to Burundi. I preached and taught, and spent time in fellowship with our African partners there. Sue and I were preparing to become the overseers of this ministry, since our staff missionaries who had been managing it had to retire due to health reasons. The partners in Burundi are good solid believers who pastor churches, run a school for the blind and a school for the deaf, train pastors, and help widows and orphans. We have a part in all of these activities. Our child sponsorship program funds the schools and the orphans programs. We send men from the United States to train pastors, and we help fund the training center there. We also help the church planters as they go farther out to remote villages to start new works. On this Burundi trip, I got to travel to fourteen different village churches. The travel was long and very rough, but I felt really well. I had recovered from the ordeal the previous year, and was delighted to be back visiting villages.

Two weeks after I arrived home from Burundi, I was working in my home office. It was a beautiful fall afternoon, and I decided to make the long walk up our drive way to get the mail. The driveway is long, and we often drive the distance, but the day was nice and I felt as good as I had felt in quite a while. As I walked out the door, I passed through a massive web that an industrious spider had taken all morning to weave. Instinctively, I swatted at the air with my hands, trying to get the silk strands out of my face. They always seem to stick like they are glued. As I stepped forward, my foot came down half on and half off the concrete porch. While the porch was only elevated a few inches off of the gravel drive, it was enough of a drop to cause me to fall straight forward and face down onto the driveway. I found myself lying in the driveway, with the certainty that my left wrist was broken. My immediate thought was to the TV commercial about the woman who has fallen and cries out to the telephone operator, "Help! I've fallen and can't get up." Could I get up? I had absolutely no trouble getting up. Now that I was up, what should I do? I walked back onto the porch and sat down on the glider. I called Sue, who had just arrived to visit her aunt who lived about an hour away. She called the orthopedic clinic and made arrangements for me to go to the office. She then called one of our staff members to drive me there. She called me back and told me the arrangements. All of the things she did were things I should have done by myself. I am not sure why I didn't do them. I do know now, however, that my education on trusting the Lord rather than trusting my own strength was going to be taken to the next level.

Friday afternoons in an orthopedic office can be very hectic. A line was formed to check in, and I patiently waited my turn. Others got into line behind me. When I came up to the front desk to check in, I was asked to present my insurance card. It was in my wallet in my back pocket. I have thousands of times reached back with my left hand and retrieved my wallet. This time, I could not. I was starting to see just how incapacitating this break was going to be. In order to accomplish this and keep the line moving, I had to get my staff member, Govinda, to retrieve the wallet for me. I was also given an iPad with a series of forms on it that needed to be completed. I went to the waiting area and sat down. My right hand could do all of the typing, but I would need my left hand to hold the iPad while

I typed. I awkwardly balanced the iPad on my knees and typed as best I could. Govinda was finally called upon once more to help complete this task. After the long wait, I went in to an examination room. Once my identity was confirmed, I was asked why I was there. I replied, "Because my wrist is broken." I was taken to an X-ray room, where pictures of my wrist were taken from a variety of painful angles. I was ushered back to the examination room, and after a bit of time, a doctor came in. We once again went through the question of why I was here, and my answer about having a broken wrist. The doctor then looked at the x-rays and pronounced, "You have a broken wrist." I remembered another trip to the orthopedic doctor ten years earlier when I had a broken finger. On that occasion, the doctor commented that I had a broken finger and he was certain it hurt very much. Both of those astute diagnoses I knew all too well, and I was well aware on this day that my wrist was broken. The question of what to do was finally addressed. On Monday morning, I would report to the hospital, and a surgeon would install an external stabilizing bar, held in place by four titanium screws. Being one who always expects the worst case scenario, my brain raced into considering all of the horrors that this would certainly involve. To get me through the weekend, my wrist was wrapped in a soft wrap, and I was given a bottle of pills, which I ultimately tossed because of their side effects.

Early Monday morning, I reported for surgery. In addition to the general anesthesia, I also had my entire left arm injected with a medication that shut down everything in the arm for the next forty-eight hours. This would be appreciated during the two days after the surgery. The surgery went well, and I was soon back at home. I was unable to use the arm for anything for about four or five days. I quickly learned why we have two arms. Routine daily tasks were made impossible for me. I also learned how much we need each other in times of trouble.

Two months later the surgeon pronounced my wrist had healed enough to remove the screws. The removal of the screws was done by a nurse in an examination room at the orthopedic office. Her medical instrument was a torque screwdriver. Each of the four screws had to be loosened from its tight grip to the inside of the bones in my arm, and each of these sent a huge jolt of pain up my arm all the way to my shoulder. After a couple months of physical therapy, I was back using both hands quite well. I use the experience of the unusable arm as an illustration when I teach on the importance of every member of a church doing his or her part to help.

A Time to Laugh and a Time to Cry

Life changes come very quickly and from a lot of directions when a person is in his late eighties and early nineties. The time came when Whitney, my parents late in life adopted daughter, left home. She went to pursue education and relationships, like young adults all over the country do every day. On the surface, my dad projected an attitude that everything was okay. Those of us, who knew him well, knew that everything was not okay. As if that wasn't enough of a challenge, the day came when he lost his driver's license. We had worried about him for quite a while. He was driving into his office one morning and side swiped a car. He didn't stop, but went on to his office. The other car phoned the police and followed him to the office. The policeman told him that he would be required to mail in his license, and sure enough, a letter from the DMV came a few days later *ordering* him to do just that. His first reaction was that he didn't need a license to drive. He had been driving for nearly eighty years and knew what he was doing. His eye sight and reflexes, however, were not up to the task. After a lot of prodding, my son Mike and my dad's office manager convinced him to sell his car. The office manager now added driver to her list of duties, and maintained that position for the balance of Dad's life. At the same time, my dad's ability to remember and comprehend things really started waning rapidly. He also had to search for words to the extent that it was difficult sometimes to get the full meaning of what he was saying. He would have some days that were more difficult than others. The frustration of his inabilities was very draining on him. It also made him more demanding and irritable. We would learn to live with all of this, but it was taxing.

The time came that I had been dreading. Dad, who was now living alone, needed help with day to day tasks. As a man who had a business, he was very used to "hiring" people to take care of things for him. He hired a woman who had been a house cleaner for him, to pick up some additional household chores like meal preparation and laying out the pills that he needed to take. She would come by in the evenings, do a little cleanup, then prepare a meal, and lay out his next day's medicine. Soon, the decision was made by this woman that she would take up residence in one of the spare bedrooms, so that she could be available at night if any emergency cropped up with my dad. This all sounds good. It was, however, anything but good. I came into my dad's office one day and he was talking with his office manager and one of my daughters. As I walked into the conference room where they were sitting, I overheard him say, "Someone should tell her to get out!" Naturally, coming in at the middle of the conversation, I needed to be brought up to speed. The woman Dad had hired was speaking abusively to him and not providing adequate meals for him. She came and went as she pleased, and would not do things that she was asked to do. What was needed was a family member to fire this woman, and develop a better situation for Dad's care. I was the one person who was equipped to do so. I drove out to my dad's house and told the woman that we would no longer need her services. She took great offense at this, but it was not an issue that was open for discussion. It was a decision that was settled. As an administrator at heart, I very much understood that when I fire someone, I now own a problem that this person was hired to solve. The most straight forward solution seemed to be bringing on board one of the elder care agencies who provide screened and bonded helpers for people like my dad who live alone and need a little extra help with household and personal care. I was able to turn this around very quickly, and the first day the helper came, everything seemed to go flawlessly. From there, it all slid downhill. The next day, his office manager picked up my Dad like she usually did, and they spent the day at his office. She dropped him off at home that evening, and told him that the agency's helper would be there very soon. When the helper showed up, it was not the same woman that had been there the night before. Instead, it was a young man. My dad had the doors locked and refused to let the man in. I received a call from the agency reporting all of this. When I called my dad, he was very angry and upset. He really didn't remember that we had told him about the helpers who would be coming. He didn't want strangers coming into his house. Long story short, our solution to the problem wasn't going to work. We now were left with two choices. Dad could move in with me or one of his grandchildren, or we could find a good assisted living community for him. After really talking this through with him, we came to the conclusion that at this point it would be better to find an assisted living community that he might like.

In the midst of the problems of care and housing, my dad began to lose a lot of weight. We thought that this was due to a lack of proper diet. We made sure he ate at the office, but we were not sure about supper time. He also became weaker. He had been treated for a lot of skin cancers, and was referred to the University of Virginia Medical facility for work on a skin cancer that seemed beyond the expertise of our local doctors. While there, we had to walk from one building to another, then back to get tests and consult with the doctor. The skin cancers proved to be less difficult than first thought, but the doctor became concerned about a lymph node. When he learned that Dad had lost a lot of weight, he ordered tests to check for Lymphoma. As I drove Dad home from the exhausting day at the medical facility, he barely had enough energy to talk. He did not want to go back there. He was willing to be tested in Lynchburg for the Lymphoma. We scheduled an appointment with the oncologist who had treated my mom. She had tests done which revealed that my dad did not have Lymphoma. She did start him on an antibiotic because she suspected he had pneumonia. Indeed, after two courses of the antibiotic, Dad started gaining some of his weight back, and being a little more energetic. At our follow up appointment, the doctor brought up the topic of assisted living. She spoke strongly to my dad about how it would benefit him. It certainly made sense to me. From the doctor's perspective, my dad needed the medical supervision as well as the personal care he would get.

We talked with my dad, and finally convinced him to go and look at an assisted living facility. We sat talking with the social worker who did admissions there, and my dad seemed to connect with her quite well. In the course of the conversion, my dad told her, "I guess I am going to be living here with you." All the arrangements were made, and we moved my dad into a beautiful apartment with two bedrooms, a living room, bathroom and a kitchenette. Per the instructions of the social worker, we brought his bed room furniture and his favorite chair from his house. I am not sure that he ever understood that this was his stuff from his house, but he did feel right at home with it, immediately.

Over the months leading up to his moving, my dad's dementia had become more and more noticeable to those around him. My dad's type of dementia was such that he would have some days where he seemed almost normal, and other days that were very difficult for him. We celebrated his ninetieth birthday about seven weeks after he arrived at the assisted living facility. Many of his friends and business contacts came to the party we held. He was having one of his better days that day and it was a great blessing to him and to all of his family.

As time progressed, my dad began to have more deterioration in memory and other cognitive skills. He had trouble getting the correct words out, and would often use wrong names or even attribute wrong actions to people. A kind of paranoia began to form, which seemed to be fed by strange dreams at night. It became harder and harder to speak about anything on more than a very shallow level. A fierce sense of motivation and independence still burned within my dad's heart. These had served him well for ninety years, and had helped make him quite successful. Now, they fought against the assistance that he really needed and others wanted to give to him. He viewed every kind offer of help as a belittlement. He came to view his apartment at the assisted living community as a jail, both figuratively and literally. As someone who had always been very secretive about his financial affairs, he totally shut down any and all attempts to help him deal with things that were now too complex for him to understand. This fact coupled with his poor eyesight made him a huge target for people who wanted to take advantage of him.

In his last few months, Dad developed a very disturbing sleep disorder. He had very vivid dreams of things that both scared him and angered him. Most afternoons when I visited him in his room, he would be asleep in his chair. He often took naps at his office in the morning. Looking back, it seemed that his sleep pattern was to get two or three hours of sleep at a time, but never any extended amount. How much of this was caused by the dreams is hard to say. None of us knew all what was going on in his brain. He had become very guarded with everything, and what he wanted to express became harder and harder to discern, because he had trouble both choosing words and remembering the full content of the thought long enough to fully express it.

My frustration level was off the charts. I wanted to step in and manage every part of Dad's life. I wanted to see the efficiency with which he had always conducted his business continue. I wanted to see him get all of the medical care he needed. At every turn, I got resistance and anger. Even things like his bookkeeping, which I had done for him for many years; he no longer wanted me to do. He declined medical visits, one by one, because "the doctors were no good" or "were wasting his time." I learned to step back and see some scenarios play out with bad results, but I kept a safety net out to make sure he didn't get hurt badly. He was happy going to his office each day and having a sense that he was doing something. He really did not care about the results. He just wanted to be the same person that he had been for the last fifty plus years. To the best extent that I possibly could, I gave him that gift.

I also came to understand just how much he missed my mom. He longed for the sense of security that only she could have provided. I see in my own life how much I miss Sue when our ministry sets us apart for just a few weeks. There are so many little things about our spouses that we do not realize are so important until that spouse is absent. I anticipate Sue's return from her ministry trips with such a great longing in my heart. I do, however, expect to see her again. For Dad, that expectation was not there- this side of heaven. His emotional strength and his cognitive abilities to reason his way through the absence were also depleted. The pain, the loneliness and the fear were left, and these were terrible companions.

The year 2016 came in with a full schedule for me. Sue and I took one of our rare trips together. We traveled to Ghana for a week. We visited our lead pastor and our ministries there. The little free school program that had started in the church had grown to well over a hundred students. These were children who could not afford books and uniforms required by the government schools. The church was offering a great service to the people of this community. People's hearts were opened to the Gospel because they saw that the Christians really cared about them. While there, I did our first pastor training in Ghana. In each of our countries, the needs and training levels are a little different. I like to personally work with the church leaders early on to help determine just what they need us to do. The most critical time of early training sessions is the question and answer period at the end. I had just spent a day outlining the concept of a healthy church and how it grows. Questions came from the trainees about this topic. Gradually, the questions became very culture specific. This is where I wanted to be. I want to know what struggles these leaders face in their own churches and in their daily lives. I firmly believe that God's Word speaks to us on a personal level in addition to on a theological level. The senior pastor was very pleased with the training, and his only question was, "When will the next training session be?" We will definitely work on that!

I also stepped in as a sort of last minute replacement teacher for our Nepal Pastor Training Program. A teacher from our church was to have been accompanied by another man who was unable to go. Since the teacher going had some medical issues, we would not send him alone. I was happy to make the trip. We were tasked with teaching the book of I Samuel. The teaching of this book went well, and the trainees asked if I would teach some out of the book of Revelation. For those who have taught this book before, they know that it is perhaps the most difficult book of the Bible to teach, because of the prophetic imagery that it contains. Once again, I was amazed at how the Lord opened the understanding of all of us, myself included. My co-teacher had several days where his medical issues really made his life miserable. Nepal's environment is difficult enough when one is feeling well. He bravely made it to the end, however. I was blessed with a very effective time with the church leaders I have been teaching for many years now. I returned home ready to face whatever challenges that I would face there-and face them I would.

The pending events that would occur in the next twelve months would keep me stateside and very much tied up. We don't know what God has waiting around the corner for us. We do know, however, that He promised to be with us as the events unfold.

The Beginning of the End

Monday afternoon, May 16, 2016, Mike, Jr. and I went to visit my dad together as we had done many times before. He talked with us, in a manner to which we had grown accustomed this past year and a half. He forgot earlier portions of the conversation, and asked many of the same questions several times. "Had we heard from Whitney?" "Was Sue traveling again?" He had a little more confusion than usual, and did his usual searching for words as he formed his thoughts.

He had also lost a lot of weight. I had recognized this some months ago, and had referred him for a medical consult. We were giving him special nutritional supplements daily, and trying to encourage him to eat anything. The nurse practitioner even suggested bedtime snacks and any variety of other things which most of us must avoid, so we will not gain weight! I noticed he was not even eating his peanut butter crackers which had been a favorite of his since before I was born. His clothing was way too big for him, and his face and arms appeared gaunt. I wondered what might be happening.

Mike and I had a good visit with him, and left around 4:30 which was approaching his supper time. He walked with his walker to the end of the hall with us where Mike and I had to get on the elevator. We hugged him and said good bye, not realizing that this was the last time we would see him up, moving around, and communicating freely.

I had been home a little more than two hours, when I got a call from the nurse at the assisted living community. My dad was complaining of severe abdominal pain, and they were having him transported to the hospital. They guessed that he might have a urinary tract infection. When I talked to the hospital nurse, she indicated that he was resting well and that they were keeping him overnight. There was not a need for me to make the trip over then, so I waited until the next morning. I sent out this short e mail about "Pap" as the grandchildren called him,:

Pap was admitted to the hospital this evening with a urinary tract infection. He is in stable condition and will be evaluated in the morning for return to the assisted living community. DAD

I arrived early the next morning. Dad had eaten a little breakfast, and had a little coffee. He was sitting up in his bed and talked a little. I found the doctor working in a cubicle out in the area of the nurse's station. He was waiting on the complete test results, but felt like the initial assessment of a urinary tract infection was likely correct. The doctor wanted to keep my dad a second night, in order to start an antibiotic. When I returned the second day, my dad was up sitting in a chair. He, once again, had eaten a little breakfast. I had found the doctor already as I was coming in. As I talked with him, he confirmed that my dad did have a urinary tract infection, but he also had a second bacterium. We needed to find its origin. The doctor started a broad spectrum antibiotic that would work against both types of bacteria. The tests required would be scheduled. I sent this e mail to the family:

I talked to the doctor this morning about Pap. The blood culture they did yesterday came back positive for a type of bacteria which could be pretty dangerous, especially for someone his age. The concern is that this type can attach itself to a heart valve, and cause big problems. They also believe that his increased confusion might be related to the bacteria. They have started him on an antibiotic which should help eliminate the bacteria. They are getting a consultation today from an infectious disease specialist. He will decide what additional steps might be necessary. Other than his increased confusion and some combativeness with the staff there, Pap seems about the same as always.

He will be at the hospital at least until tomorrow, to facilitate the medications and the consultation with the other doctor. DAD

The next day, Dad met the infectious disease specialist. She was there when I arrived at the hospital. My dad said that she was a worker there, and was nineteen years old. The doctor, who was in her forties, took no offense. She dealt well with my dad's confusion. I wrote this e mail to the family:

I talked with two doctors at the hospital this morning. They both shared the same information. Yesterday, another blood culture was run on Pap. It showed two different bacteria in his blood. They have been doing heavy duty IV antibiotics, of a broad spectrum type, to address both bacteria types. They are going to culture again today. They did a CT scan of his lower abdomen yesterday and found nothing conclusive. They were looking to find where the bacteria might be coming from. It is a kind of bacteria that normally exists in one's digestive and urinary tracts, but does not reside in the blood. The one doctor who is an infectious disease specialist has ordered a sonogram of Pap's heart valve today. Their biggest concern is that these bacteria might connect themselves to the heart. Pap looked much better today, but was extremely verbally hyperactive. He mixes up a lot of names and places, and jumps from one thought to the next in mid-sentence. He talked non-stop while I was there, even when the doctor was trying to listen to his heart and lungs. Well, you all know what I know now. I will write again if anything new comes up. DAD

The doctor wanted an ultra-sound of my dad's heart, to determine if the bacteria might be connected to that organ. The strain of bacteria found in my dad's blood was often associated with heart valves. The test did, in fact, suggest that a heart valve might be involved, but the test was not conclusive. It was recommended that another test be performed using an ultra-sound inside of an endoscopic tube inserted down his throat. This sounded dangerous and uncomfortable to me, but the doctors felt that the best antibiotic could not be administered, without confirmation of the bacteria being in the heart valve. In looking back on this time, I can see how the anxiety about his condition was impacting my dad. His mental confusion prevented him from understanding or even remembering what the doctors told him. He knew he was sick, but could not comprehend that the medical personnel were trying hard to get him well.

The next day, as I arrived at the nurses' station, I was told that the radiology people were on their way up to get my dad for the difficult test. My dad was also exhibiting some symptoms of pneumonia, so the doctor wanted a chest X-ray as well. They wanted me to accompany him down to the lab. My dad was asleep. He had a rough night. As is the case with elderly people, he often experienced sleep disturbances. I was glad he was sleeping, but I knew he would need to be awake for the test. I quickly sent off this e mail to the family:

Pap is heading down for a procedure now. I will try to let you know when it is done. DAD

When we arrived in the Radiology Department of the hospital, we were taken into a room. A nurse came in and gave us a very thorough description of what the procedure would be like. My dad seemed to take all of this in. The nurse then gave him a throat numbing gargle to use. My dad basically just swallowed it, but I was assured by the nurse that this was not a problem. I must have had a really worried look on my face. The nurse began to assure me that they would discontinue the test if my dad experienced any discomfort, or if the tube met with any resistance as it went down. The doctor, a heart specialist, came in and went over the procedure with us again, giving me the same reassurances. When everything was prepped, I was escorted to a waiting area. I sat and prayed. I opened the Bible App on my phone, and read Psalm 62:5-8. I posted this Bible reference on Facebook, knowing that many of my good friends would know this as a distress call and would pray. They did! After about half an hour that seemed like an eternity, the doctor came into the waiting area and told me that the procedure was finished and that Dad had done very well. The doctor was very pleased, because he had been able to conclusively diagnose that the bacteria problem was associated with a leaking heart valve. I had mixed relief and happiness to know there was a treatable problem. This would turn out, ironically to be very sad news in the end. I wrote the following e mail to the family:

Doctor did a procedure called a T.E.E. which puts a tube down the esophagus to do a sonogram of the heart. The test revealed a leak in a heart valve which is the place where the bacteria is entering. The good news is that no surgery will be needed. He will, however, need a strong antibiotic for an extended period of time. He will likely be here for the weekend. Thanks for praying for him. DAD

My thinking at the time was that a few days of IV antibiotics and a prescription for an extended course of pills and he would be up and around and back at the assisted living home by early the following week. This was not to be. As I visited the hospital each day that week, Dad did not appear to be getting stronger. He had also stopped eating most things and slept more. In short, my expectation that the strong antibiotics would quickly knock out the infection, were proven totally wrong. The doctors now told me that he would have to have IV antibiotics for 4-6 weeks. They further said that he would need to be transferred to a different hospital, where he could get a full range of care and have the proper nursing staff to administer the antibiotics. Two things needed to happen before the move, however. First, they needed to install a PIC Line, which is a port installed in a larger vein near the clavicle. This facilitates the IV treatments. Secondly, he needed to recover a little strength so he could make the trip to the other hospital. By week's end, the port was installed.

Sue and I left that Friday for a long weekend out of town. Since I felt reassured that we had moved forward on my dad's path to recovery, I felt like this would not be a problem. Mike and Whitney were keeping an eye on things. Additionally his office manager/helper was coming every day instead of going into the office. My dad's maintenance man, who had also become my dad's good friend, spent goodly amounts of time with him. I would be five and half hours away, but free to drop everything and return home if needed. I sent the following e mail to Mike and Whitney:

Mom and I will be out of town half a day on Friday, all day Saturday and Sunday, and part of Monday. I will look in on Pap Friday morning and see if the doctor has any updates. If either of you could drop by on Saturday or Sunday, that would be good. He slept through my visit today, and didn't really know I was there the day before. The doctor was commenting on how extended stays in the hospital are very hard on older people. They get greater dementia from it, and other circulation related problems. They want to get him up some, but the nurses said he was unable to stand when they tried to take him to the bathroom. The hospital wants to transfer him to the other hospital for his IV meds and rehab as soon as possible. The absolute earliest it could be is Friday, but with Memorial Day weekend, it is likely to be next week. If they do happen to transfer him, it would be good if one of you stops in the new place. I will be in touch by my phone while we are gone, and could rush home in an emergency. Thanks for looking out for Pap. DAD

As I was on the road, I received a call from the hospital, telling me that there was an available bed at the other hospital beginning on Sunday. They would let me know if and when they were going to transfer my dad. I wrote the following e mail to Mike and Whitney:

Hospital has a bed opening up on Sunday at the other hospital where they want to transfer Pap. If he is strong enough to go they will transport him. If not, they will keep him where he is. DAD

I had been noticing a drastic increase in the amount of time that my dad was sleeping. Both my dad and I are physiologically hardwired to almost hibernate when we are very sick. This was a definite red flag that something was going on. His lack of strength was another tip off. Until this past week, he had vigorously resisted anyone's help doing personal tasks. Now, he couldn't do any of these without help at every step.

On Saturday, I got a call from one of the hospital's staff doctors. It brought very sobering news. I wrote this e mail to all of the family:

I talked with the hospital doctor this morning. He is concerned about

Pap's continuing confusion. He also said that Pap's white blood count was up today. This can indicate more infection or may just be a one-time event. They are checking it regularly. Pap needs to get stronger in order to be moved to the rehab unit. DAD

Sue and I decided to leave Sunday morning and return home. I was very uneasy about my dad's condition. His struggle had also taken on another enemy: pneumonia. His inability to get food down his esophagus had the really bad consequence of causing food and beverage to suck down into his lungs. This aspiration was the genesis of the lung disorder. Dad's already weakened body was doing its best to throw off this disease, as it had thrown off so many others in the past ninety-one years, but the deck was stacked against it. The other infections were already overtaxing his immune system. The antibiotics were not keeping up with the rapid replication of the bacteria. He was weak from not ingesting enough calories, and his breathing was hindered. He was fighting gamely, but it would take a miracle of God to overcome everything that was coming down on him. Dad was not getting better; he was getting worse. He was not going to be back on his feet in a couple of days. It would take weeks, if it happened at all. There are times in our lives where we can't even formulate a prayer that makes sense to us. How wonderful is it that God understands our cries and needs fully, even when we do not?

A call from the doctor came on Sunday while we were in route home. The doctor indicated that my dad's white count was down a little, but still very elevated. His temperature seemed to have come back into the normal range, so I felt a little glimmer of optimism. That was short lived. The doctor emphasized the seriousness of Dad's condition. He made the statement that he just wanted us to be prepared. He didn't say prepared for what, but it was crystal clear what we needed to be prepared to see happen.

Monday through Wednesday of that week were full of continued blood tests, doctors listening to lungs, blood pressure cuffs squeezing a sore arm, and much activity around Dad. One of the last intelligible things Dad communicated to me was his discomfort and unhappiness with the constant barrage of needles, nurses, lab techs, and doctors who were accosting him. He could not form all of the words, but I could read the hand gestures and see the anguish on his face. He was hurting, scared, agitated, and confused. *It broke my heart.*

I was still holding on to the hope that six weeks of powerful antibiotics would turn things around for my dad. On Thursday, the doctor pretty much took away all of my hope. I explained it to the family in this e mail:

I spoke with the doctor a few minutes ago. He was having trouble finding words to say about Pap's condition and prognosis. Pap still faces six weeks of antibiotics in order to eliminate his heart infection. His temperature is back down from the other infections, so those seem to be under control. His lungs are very congested and he really doesn't have the strength to cough up much. He has to have oxygen all of the time. He keeps pulling out the nose clip delivering the oxygen, and his oxygen level dropped to 60% this morning from where he had pulled out the clip last night. His most severe problem now is his inability to swallow food or liquids. The therapist tried again today to help him, but the fluids go into his lungs, so they can't give him anything. The doctors had hoped that this might reverse itself, but it has not. The combination of infections and lack of nutrition will, of course, make it impossible for him to last long term. We have the option of inserting a feeding tube down his throat to deliver nutrition. Many people do not tolerate these well, and given that he is pulling out a tiny, non-invasive nose clip for oxygen, it is a certainty that he would constantly be pulling out the feeding tube. This would necessitate restraining him, which is essentially tying his hands down to the bed. The doctor said that he cannot promise that Pap could ever recover back to any kind of normal life. There is not a good path out. From the times I have been there each day, he recognizes some of us, but he doesn't really understand what is going on. He also will wander off talking about people from many years ago, or try to get out of bed to go somewhere. He is unable to stand up now. The doctor shared that he doesn't think Pap will last the full six weeks it will take to administer all of the antibiotics that he needs. They are going to continue all of his necessary meds to ensure he is comfortable and reasonably pain free, but medications like his cholesterol pills they are stopping, since they are near impossible to get him to swallow, and they are not going to help him in the short term. There are no good, happy paths to take from here. We can pray for a miracle from God, and we can pray that God eases his journey if He chooses to take him on home. If you can go by and see him, that is good to do. He may speak with you, or he may not know you are there. Don't get too down. We all are sad to see Pap in such bad shape. The promise of heaven is sure, however, and soon he will wake up healthy, and reunited with those who have gone on before. DAD

I had now talked with three different doctors from the hospital. I had very pointedly inquired as to any path that might exist for my dad to recover to any level of functioning at all. None of them gave me any hope. It was recommended that we bring in hospice, since they were best equipped to give my dad the best level of comfort and dignity during these final days of his life. I met that afternoon with a nurse practitioner and a doctor from hospice. If someone had joined us mid conversation, they might have assumed that I was upset with the doctor. I was very aggressively grilling her about the options that might remain for my dad. I was trying to walk a line that on one side held out hope for a miraculous recovery, and on the other side made Dad comfortable, pain free, and in a place where those of us who loved him could get our last few days with him. The meds could not work in the short amount of time he had remaining. They required daily taking of blood and culturing it, and created a lot of intrusion into his space. They would be discontinued. He could not get enough oxygen breathing on his own, so the oxygen would be continued. Decisions like these are clear cut in their logical, intellectual consideration. They are very painful and difficult to make at one's gut level, because the choices all end with great sorrow in the long term. Essentially, it requires acknowledging that one is not capable of doing the thing he most passionately wants to do at this point: save Dad's life. Before him stands a problem with no solution. Despite many people's noble efforts, despite his noble efforts, Dad is going to die. How often have I made the global statement, "We all are going to die someday," in a very matter of fact manner? It is very easy to talk about death in those terms. It is not so easy when one is really facing the death of a loved one. I look back now and greatly appreciate the professionalism of this doctor, as well as the other doctors with whom I communicated during these difficult days.

The decision was made to transfer Dad to the hospice unit at the other hospital. The next day, I had to sign a number of papers, which relieved the hospital from liability for not hooking up feeding tubes or keeping my dad's vitals running artificially. Even though he had signed an advanced directive stating this many years ago, I had to affirm that this was what he had desired in such a situation. It is far easier to make a good rational decision about death when one is not looking into death's ominous eyes. On Friday evening, June 3, 2016, my dad was transported to the hospice unit. There is a small bit of bitter irony in this date. June 3, 2016 marked the thirteenth anniversary of the founding of Allow The Children. My dad's influence on my life played a role in this organization's founding and operation. Now, on this date, he was being transported to the place where he would live out his final days on planet earth.

Dad was a bit agitated during the transport. He had been trying to get people to leave him alone for the last week and a half, so this was not surprising. As soon as he got into the bed at the hospice unit, he calmed down, and was never agitated again for the rest of his few days. I wrote the following e mail to the family:

Pap is being transported to Hospice 1 at the other hospital. This is the hospice unit there. After consulting with two doctors today, they could not see a path by which Pap could recover to even close to where he was. He is unable to eat or drink because his esophagus won't let food down, and anything going into his mouth goes into his lungs. The infections would require another six weeks of IV antibiotics, but the doctors don't see Pap lasting that long. Administering the antibiotics requires regular blood testing, and Pap has been fighting against the discomfort of this for over a week now. We discussed a feeding tube. Pap had left an end of life health care directive saying he did not want one. The doctors feel that he would not tolerate it, and it would cause him great discomfort. His body seems to be shutting down naturally. His extremities are cold, and his finger nails are taking on a bluish color. His veins are not pushing the fluids the way they should. Our objective now is to keep him pain free and as comfortable as possible. The medications, needles sticking him, day and night nurses taking vital signs, and other things he has been enduring for the past two weeks will be stopped. They would be necessary if the rest of the body was bouncing back, but it isn't, so there is no need to put him through any more discomfort. At Hospice 1, they will have 24/7 care and the ability to give meds for pain or to help him with breathing, which has been difficult for him this past week. They have also told me that any of us can call to ask questions. I have not been there yet, but I am told that Hospice 1 is just across the four way intersection from the parking garage, and there are signs. Strange as it sounds, you will have to go up the stairs from the parking lot to get to the first floor where his room will be. DAD

The Dark Journey to the Light

I arrived early on Saturday morning to the hospice unit, and approached the nurse's station. Upon inquiring, I was directed to my dad's room. The rooms were old, concrete block walled rooms in a building that dated back to the Second World War. They had been nicely modernized, into spacious and warm patient rooms. My dad was sleeping and unaware of his surroundings. A doctor came in shortly after I arrived. She said she was the doctor on call for the weekend. After listening to Dad's heart and doing some adjustments to his oxygen tubes, she departed. My dad looked very peaceful as he lay sleeping. I suppose I expected him to awaken at any moment, and we would converse. He did not. After several hours, I needed a break. Sitting doing nothing, but wishing you could do something, exacts a physical and emotional toll. I left for a few hours, and then returned. Nothing had changed, and would not change for a week. As evening came, I left for home. I told the nurse at the desk that if anything at all happened during the night, she should call me. She assured me that she would do so.

Sue had departed a day earlier with a team of ladies heading to Guatemala to minister there. Sue is my emotional strength, and after the first day on this "death watch," I really missed her. I was a bundle of emotions, most of which I could not sort out or even start to understand. When one is looking helplessly on as a cherished family member is wasting away, it is very difficult. If that loved one was your leader, your mentor, and your example as a husband and father, one feels an added vulnerability. My thoughts turned to how much like my dad that I was. It crossed my mind that I might be seeing a preview of my future. Would my son be making my medical decisions and sitting by my bedside as I slipped out of this world?

Sunday morning saw me make an early run to check on Dad. Even though the drive was thirty minutes from my home, I wanted to see him before I went to church. The oft repressed optimist in me hoped that my dad, who was a notorious early riser, would be awake, sitting up, and ready to talk. Like he had been all of the day before, he was sleeping. I spent about an hour by his bedside, and headed to church. So many of my good friends at church who knew my dad was in the hospital, asked me about how he was doing. I found myself intellectually answering that he was near death. Each of my friends was very encouraging to me. I had not emotionally come to grips yet with what my intellect had grasped. My dad *was* near death. I drove back to the hospice unit after church. The afternoon went pretty much like the previous one. Dad continued sleeping. Doctors and nurses came in often and checked on him. A caring nurse's aide came and bathed him. Teams of aides would turn him regularly and adjust the height of the bed. The care was everything one could ask for. A hospital chaplain came by to ask if I had a church and/or a spiritual caregiver. I did, but I appreciated her care and concern. The course of this day was the course of the remaining five days as well. I would spend as much time as I could, would take a few hours break, then return and stay until evening. This journey was done with a number of friends coming by and visiting. Like me, Whitney and my dad's office manager were there every day as well. Most days, Dad's pastor, Pastor Clarkson came by for a while. He would read scripture and pray with us, and his natural pleasant and joyful disposition was very uplifting. Ironically, the pastor of my own church had left for a sabbatical the day that Dad was admitted to the hospital. He was not available during this time at all. The Lord, who hears my cries of suffering, saw fit to bring Pastor Clarkson around as His reminder that He had not forsaken me.

Monday was a repeat of the previous day. There was a lot of sitting helplessly, as Dad lay sleeping. All the staff did their job, Pastor Clarkson came by, Dad's office manager and Whitney were there, and absolutely no change occurred.

On Tuesday, a different doctor came in early. After her examination of my dad, she said, "he will not last much longer." I inquired as to how much longer, and she replied, "Only a few more hours." This was emotionally disturbing on the one hand, but emotionally relieving on the other hand. We watched and waited for the rest of the day, fully expecting each breath that he took to be his last. At the end of the day, however, his breaths, though very shallow, were still as regular as they had been that morning. As I left, I once again asked the nurse to call me if any change at all occurred. I went home, expecting that at some point that night I would get the call saying that my dad had passed. I connected on FaceTime with Sue that evening. While I was happy to hear her voice and see her face, I could only relate the doctor's prediction, and the continued waiting. Sue, apparently saw the anguish I was going through, and also could sense that even though Dad's passing did not happen on this day, it was going to be soon. I did not know it at the time, but she went on line after talking with me, and changed her return ticket to be back on Thursday night instead of Sunday morning. Based on the doctor's prognosis, we had talked to Pastor Clarkson about having my dad's graveside service on Saturday morning and his celebration of life service on Monday morning. My youngest son, Tommy, was leaving Saturday afternoon for a two week military obligation, so we were planning to enable him to attend his grandfather's funeral right before he would leave. Pastor Clarkson was also scheduled the following week for an out of town revival meeting, so we wanted to make sure he could be there to do the service.

On Wednesday morning, Dad was still breathing. Whitney, his office manager and I sat at bedside like we had been doing for the past several days. The doctor's evaluation had nothing new. I watched his breathing and marveled how long there was between shallow breathes. Dad's body was continuing a slow process of shutting itself down a little at a time. I left a little early, but came back in the evening, when I could be all alone with my dad. I talked to him, and I cried over him. I wanted so badly to see him wake up, talk to me, and be himself once again. Thursday morning was a repeat of Wednesday morning. Tommy was very upset. He asked if he should try to be released from his military obligation to stay here for his grandfather's last days. I assured him that his "Pap" would tell him to take care of business with his military obligation. Reluctantly, the next day, he departed, knowing in his heart that he would not see Pap again. I came back to the hospital again in the evening, and once again talked to Dad and wished that there was something I could do to change the circumstances. I could not help but wonder if over these last five weeks, was there a point at which I should have told the doctors, "Try something else." Had I missed something, or had the large team of medical professionals missed something that should have been caught? Should I have insisted that all possible life support mechanisms be brought into play, and all heroic measures taken to prolong Dad's life as long as possible? I had made the best decision that could be made with all of the facts that I had, but did I miss something? Even right decisions do not lift the weight of the burden off of our shoulders. We can live knowing we have made the best decision we could have made, but we can never really walk away unscarred.

On Friday morning, Whitney, Dad's office manager and I once again arrived. There was no question that fatigue was great among us. Waiting in a stressful situation is exhausting. The doctor, who had predicted that Dad's death would happen on Tuesday, came in and did an examination. Much as she had done on Tuesday, she said, "He will only last a few more hours." This was very conflicting for me. In my own mind, I could not see him lasting another day, but I had been thinking that for a couple of days now. Further, this doctor had totally missed the mark on her prognosis Tuesday, so I didn't have a lot of confidence in her prediction. Looking back, I am thankful for these "end of life" doctors working with hospice. They entered medicine to save lives, not to usher lives out. They were all extremely compassionate to us, knowing what we were going through. Pastor Clarkson came by and shared Scripture with us. He then prayed and said that we should call him if anything happened.

By three o'clock that afternoon, I was totally dragging. I made the thirty minute drive home, took about half an hour nap, and got back in my car and drove to the hospital. I pulled into the parking lot just at 5:00 p.m. The news was just coming on the radio when I turned it off. I walked the two minutes up to Dad's room. As I entered, Whitney was leaning down kissing my dad's forehead and crying. Dad's office manager had her phone, dialing a number. The number was my number. When she saw me, she stopped dialing and said, simply, "He's gone." Dad had passed just as I pulled into the parking lot. The doctor came in, looked at her watch, and began filling out the information for the death certificate. Whitney and the office manager said good bye to Dad, and left. The death watch was over. The doctor and a social worker asked about arrangements for the body. It was strangely comfortable to fall back into the administrative mode for a few minutes. All the arrangements had already been made. I merely had to sign as his next of kin to release his body to the funeral home. The nurses all expressed their condolences to me. The social worker offered to answer any questions about what I needed to do now. I had already researched that. The big thing I had to do was to call family and Pastor Clarkson. My various family members were very consoling. Pastor Clarkson and I agreed upon times and formats for the funeral services. It sounds almost inhumane, but the relief from the long ordeal, seemed to lift a heavier burden than the sadness of the passing placed upon me. I had assured Whitney as she left that Dad was now free from pain, and in a much better place than we were. He was home! Furthermore, Mom was now reunited with the man she had loved, and Dad was now with the love of his life, free from all dementia and pain. We would join them one day in the future.

The doctors and nurses offered me some alone time with my father. I had returned to the hospital with every intention of spending time with him like I had on the previous evenings. Now, I had no desire to be there, because he was not there. My mother's exhortation came back. He was no longer in that frail body. He was in heaven.

On Sunday afternoon, we had a family time when we could all view our loved one if we chose to do so. Many family members did, but some did not. The past several months of being unable to take in adequate nutrition had left Dad's body looking like the pictures I have seen of POW's. It was quite difficult for me to see him. Better than anyone else left alive, I knew what he was supposed to look like, and had, in fact looked like only six months or so earlier. The next morning, the family, along with Pastor Clarkson, met at the graveyard. We had a short service, and left my dad's body lying next to my mom's body.

I had arranged to have the celebration of life service at our short staffed church. Pastor Brodie, our church's Executive Pastor and a member of our Allow The Children Board of Directors made all of the arrangements. Our Senior Pastor was out on sabbatical, but we could not have asked for anyone more gracious and accommodating to us than Pastor Brodie was. He participated in the service along with Pastor Clarkson, who had been my dad's pastor and very close friend. We were able to find a piano player who was very good. Our church's regular musicians were unavailable. We had a good sized crowd of people for the service. They consisted of some of our church members who were there on Sue's and my behalf, and a number of friends and business associates of Dad's from over the years. Both Mike, Jr. and I gave short testimonies describing Dad's life. His strongest legacy certainly was his kindness and giving to so many people who had great needs. The unspoken legacy, I would hope, would be a son, grandsons and granddaughters who follow Jesus Christ. Certainly the decision to follow Jesus that he made so many years earlier had impacted all of our lives.

Questions without Answers

Following my dad's funeral, there were a few administrative things which I had to take care of, but I was now back to being full time at Allow The Children. I resumed some travel, and began to consider various directional issues for the organization. At the same time, it became clear that one does not walk through a difficult end of life experience with a loved one, and return to a "normal" life without missing a step. Emotionally, there is a time of grieving, and spiritually, there is a time of self-examination. Actually, times of grief are very dangerous spiritual times. Humans seem to desire to know what happened and why it happened. They often slip into feelings of anger, guilt, or spiritual depression.

All of us, to one degree or another, like to understand what brings about the experiences in our lives. Over the centuries, philosophers, psychologists, physicians, religious leaders and academics have offered us explanations which may or may not satisfy us. Each of us has his own "world view" that filters every new event or bit of information that enters his life. That world view is shaped by our experiences and beliefs about whom or what determines our behavior. Certainly we are pre-programmed with certain built in abilities to learn basic associations. It does not take many times touching a hot stove to develop a basic understanding of how to conduct oneself around hot stoves. Even life forms much farther down on the animal kingdom chart will learn associations and approach-avoidance lessons. For animals and humans alike, this type of learning will be a lifelong process, and will afford much protection and comfort.

People, unlike animals, have the habit of following up the question

"What?" with the question "Why?" I have five children and nine grandchildren, and somewhere around the age of three or four years old, the question "Why?" begins to come up. Likewise, people who are senior citizens, like I am, also want to know the reason why things happen. My world view includes the existence of a sovereign God, who both created and interacts with this world. I believe that He created us after His own image. This included a will to make decisions, an intellect to develop wisdom and understanding, and a set of emotions to help bond us to Him and to others. This God, then, personifies an infinite will, an infinite wisdom, and an infinite bond of love with those He created. In my world view, I understand the wide range of freedom which I was given, as well as the relationship which I have with the Creator. I am able to control much of my own environment. I have learned many things and developed many skills thus far in this lifetime. There are things, however, that I seek to understand, yet never come to that understanding. The same is true of many who have a totally different world view than mine. The first course for most people is to keep searching. Indeed, we enjoy the benefit of many medical and technological breakthroughs, because someone kept searching until he understood. Since my world view includes a God who does make His presence known to His creation, my "Why?" must certainly direct itself to that God. I hear about so many people walking away from their faith in God, because they had their question of "Why?" unanswered. "Why did this happen to me? Why would a loving God allow this to happen and not intervene?" Part of learning, however, is learning when to abandon an unfruitful search. This is especially true when we ask God "Why?" Such has been my course as I consider many of the events I have described in this book.

When I look back at my mother's death, I have so many "why" questions. Why did God not let her live four more months so she could have held two new great-granddaughters who were born during that time? Why did God not let her live another year so she could have seen her adopted daughter graduate and launch in life? Why did God not let her live two more years so that she could have ministered to her mother who died in that time frame? Why did God take her out of my dad's life, leaving him sad, lonely, and without his lifelong companion that he greatly needed? Obviously these reflect things that I would have done differently if I were the sovereign God who had the power to intervene in the lives of people. I am not God, and unlike God, I do not have an infinite store of wisdom. While in my eyes, I love my mother with an enormous amount of love, I also cannot match the love that God has for her. My mother's encouragement to me in her last few weeks was to understand that she would be in the care of the Lord. I wanted only the best for the mother I loved, and she would have just that in the presence of her Lord.

I also struggled with the concept of long life as a blessing for Nanny. Her physical strength and mobility were very limited over her last ten years. There were no true peers of hers remaining, and only my mother from the generation below her. The last two years of her life, my mother was gone as well, and Nanny lived what appeared to be a purposeless life. I valued her life, but I wondered why God would extend it so much and at the same time restrict it so greatly. The Scriptures tell us that long life is a blessing, but it just didn't look like a blessing when I viewed the existence Nanny had. I have no doubt that God had a purpose. She was a blessing to me, and gave meaning to that part of my life which she touched. Her one hundred year old life was precious to God, and to her grandson as well.

I struggled with my time with my dad over the last three or four years of his life. Why would God take such a good man as Dad, who had given so much to the ministries of so many, and put him through such an unhappy end of life? Why would Dad experience the confusion and inability to express his thoughts and needs? Why could I not create a better end of life experience for him? Why would God disrupt the flow of my ministry by greatly restricting my ability to travel out of the country due to Dad's circumstances? The longer I ask these types of questions, the more I tend to come to focus upon myself. That is not where I want to live, however. God just lets me visit there, to reconnect with the truth that I really need God's grace in my life. At these critical junctions, I will either run away from God, or I will run to Him. I will either blame God for my unhappiness, or I will praise Him for His mercy and goodness in the midst of this cursed world. I will either flounder in self-pity searching for any port of comfort, or I will come through this trial, strengthened, purified, and more focused on God and His purposes for my life.

Our tendency is to ask the question, "why?" when we are not happy with what we experience. The question of "Why has God blessed me so greatly?" is not one so often asked, though it really should be. In fact, this question has presented itself to me on numerous occasions, and always points to God's purposes for me in my life. God has a place of blessing for each of us. This place of blessing might include a geographical location, but it more often is a state of mind and a perspective on our lives and our world. The blessings which God showers upon us are not because we are such good people. Indeed, it is very presumptuous to impose a debt upon God. Even if I have been the model Christ Follower- which I have not-God owes me nothing. The blessings He has given are for me to use as I minister to and seek to bless others. We often define a missionary as being one who has worked cross-culturally to bring the Gospel to others. This follows the western thinking of defining people by their vocation. A more global perspective on a missionary's identity majors on how God has blessed and equipped him, and what God's purposes are for him in this life.

I have known dozens of people over my life time who have said that they were searching for God's will in their lives. Why do we attribute such mischievous ways to the Lord? Do we really think that He creates a perfect will and purpose for our lives, and then cleverly hides it? If God put a burning bush before Moses and took Isaiah into the heavenly throne room, how much more clearly must He define His purposes for one like me? I have the scriptures which make God's will plain. I live in my world every day, and have eyes to see the needs and ears to hear the cries of the lost and hurting. In my experience, I only need to start doing what I know God has shown me and equipped me to do, and He opens the door much wider to enable me to be all the more effective. At the same time, I have struggles. All of us experience times when we ask the question, "Why God?" These struggles have destroyed countless ministries over the years. They have caused a crisis of faith in our twenty-first century North American churches. We have bought into the false doctrine that when we do something good, God owes us a reward. When we start to grasp that the Creator can use the worst of circumstances to mold us into His best equipped servants, we can live with joy in our place of blessing, even when the sky is full of the most ominous clouds of struggle.

All of us need to look back at our own lives and at the heritage passed on by those who went before us. Aging has a way of bringing such an examination to the forefront of our minds. From where did we come, and how were we brought up? What blessings has God bestowed upon us and what hardships have we been required to overcome? What are God's purposes for our lives, and how have we seen Him provide for these? As we minister to our aging parents, we must appreciate the fact that they have been God's agents for developing many different aspects of our lives. Some of us will have a very blessed time walking the final steps with our mom or dad, while others may look back on it as the most difficult times we have experienced. In my case, I had both experiences. Whatever the circumstances, we must go into them, through them, and out of them with a strong sense of the purposes of God *for* our lives and the presence of God *in* our lives.

We also must look at what we have done with the opportunities and resources God has entrusted to us. Were we wise or were we a fool? Did we love others, or did we only love self? Did we follow God's purposes or did we flee from His will for our lives? When we began Allow The Children, we never envisioned it as being significant enough to plan its existence beyond our life time. We had set aside financial reserves to support our partners for six to eight months after we departed. We trusted that our partners would have enough time to find new support for their ministries before the six to eight month reserve funds ran out. In recent years, we have moved into a second generation among our ministry partners. Some, who started as children, now are in charge of children's homes, working as evangelists, directing church programs, or participating as active members of their local church. Allow The Children is a ministry that has far outgrown our human understanding. The principles of faithfulness that we tried to honor in life, we must now try to apply as we approach our death. At the same time, we must hold on to the reality that this has always been God's plan, and He has brought it this far. If He decides to extend it after Sue and I are gone, He can and will do it.

As I look back on my life, I have been blessed. My parents and grandparents left a legacy for which I am both proud and thankful. The Lord has seen fit to open many doors of ministry to me, and I have found that He has equipped me to be a part of His greater work worldwide. When I ask the question, "Why has God blessed and equipped me in such a way?" I have found that the blessings correspond with the open doors. That set of open doors and corresponding blessings continues to manifest itself in Allow The Children.

Sue and I now must look at what will be our legacy when we are gone. Our children are all launched, with some launched more successfully than others. At this time, none of these appear to be called or equipped to lead Allow The Children, nor do they even seem bent in that direction. We are beginning the process with our Board of Directors to develop a succession plan. We must decide what they will do in the event of a sudden, emergency transition. We must also develop a plan for the long term gradual transition that must take place in all ministries. In my many years, I have seen some very effective transitions of churches and mission ministries. I also have seen some failures. Like the writer of Ecclesiastes, in the back of my mind there is the fear, and even disgust, that when I am gone, a "fool" will become the new leader of the ministry I have so loved, and he will squander all the blessings that God has heaped upon it. Intellectually, I understand that it is God's ministry, God's blessing, and God who will build up or tear down His works in His own time and at His own pleasure. It is very hard to take this knowledge out of one's intellect and get it into one's gut. I will, one day, be removed from Allow The Children Ministries. Perhaps the removal will be by death, but maybe it will be by God's call to something else. Taking small steps of faith through the years and trusting God to work His will is what brought us to where we are now. If God chooses to continue Allow The Children, He will raise up a new set of leaders who will likewise need to take small steps of faith trusting God.

When my life ends, I will rejoin the two old ladies who are now smiling in the presence of the Lord. I will also be reunited with my dad, who will once again have his joy, his wisdom, and his loving persona which had been so blunted by end of life malady. If those who come behind me look at my impact on their lives, I would hope that they would do so with the fondness that I have for the parents and grandparents who blessed my life so greatly. My life has written another chapter in a book that has no ending. While I expect to leave material blessings to family and ministry, my hope is that the footprints which I leave will shine brightly to keep them firmly on the path of faith which has been so good to me.

Be Part of the Story...

Sponsor an orphan or abandoned child Bring a Hindu, Buddhist or Muslim child into a Christian environment. The child is taught daily from God's Word and has an opportunity to trust the Lord as Savior. Most orphans still have extended family ties to which they will return some day as witnesses.

Sponsor a Pastor's child Shoulder some of the load with a village pastor, meeting the needs of his family and enabling him to minister to others. It is a huge blessing to one who may be following the call of God with no salary at all.

Sponsor a child from an impoverished believer's family Many Christian families are not able to pay the school fees for their children or to meet the basic needs of these children. Sponsorship might mean that the child can stay with his family instead of being surrendered to a children's home for survival. Sponsorship helps to produce an educated adult, well grounded in God's Word, to be a church leader and a witness in the community.

Request a child from a specific country, gender or age group. Choose from our web site (which is never a full list of children waiting), or let us assign a child who is in great need of your help.

Send a one-time gift to help with the many needs of Allow The Children You can help with special projects, training of church leaders, emergency relief work and other expenses.

Let God use you to bless others! Contact Us!

By Letter: Allow The Children P O Box 15039 Lynchburg, VA 24502
By Phone: 434-525-8866
By e-mail: sue@allowthechildren.org, mike@allowthechildren.org
By website: **www.allowthechildren.org**

Printed in the United States
By Bookmasters